SAM HOUSTON

HERO OF SAN JACINTO

SAM HOUSTON

...Painting in Texas State Capitol building, Austin

SAM HOUSTON

Hero of San Jacinto

by
Catherine Troxell Gonzalez

EAKIN PRESS ★ AUSTIN, TEXAS

FIRST EDITION

Copyright © 1983
By Catherine Troxell Gonzalez

Published in the United States of America
By Eakin Press
P.O. Box 23066, Austin, Texas 78735

ALL RIGHTS RESERVED

ISBN 0-89015-382-5

Dedication

to

Marcella Scroggins Mondrick

who has listened patiently to all my problems in writing my books and who has read my manuscripts before they were sent to the publisher.

PRESIDENT SAM HOUSTON

— Engraving by W. J. Edwards from a daguerreotype made while Houston was the first president of the Republic of Texas. Photo from New York Public Library.

General Sam Houston, Governor of Tennessee, First President of the Republic of Texas, Governor of Texas, and the Hero of San Jacinto, must have been born under an ill-fated star. His life was heroic, turbulent, and colorful. He suffered misunderstanding in Tennessee, where he resigned his office as governor, and in Texas, where he also resigned under pressure. He refused to take the Oath of Allegiance to the Confederacy because he believed too strongly in the Union to accept secession. Though he won the Battle of San Jacinto, he was censured because of his strategic retreat. In all, Houston led a star-crossed life.

Stories

For Young

Americans

CHAPTER ONE

As he came near the clearing, the young lad sighed deeply. He gazed down the green valley. It was his again. But his feet hurt. He slipped off the heavy leather shoes. He tied the thongs together and slung them over his shoulder. The grass cooled and soothed his bare feet. It was good to get back to the life he loved. Soon he would be able to see the smoke from the campfires of his friends. He wiggled his toes and rubbed his sore heel. He was humming a soft little tune.

He felt in his jacket pocket for his book. There it was, his *Iliad.* He knew most of it by heart. He loved the sound of the stately lines. Lifting his shoulders, he stood tall and slim. His friends should be here soon. They always knew when he was on his way to visit. He didn't know how they knew, but they would be at the edge of the laurel thicket waiting for him.

He wondered a second if Ma would miss him. Probably not before supper time. She knew when he missed the evening meal that the wild, free life of the Cherokees was calling him. She had become used to his being away. But she could never bring herself to accept his choice of friends.

Bending over, he cupped his hands. Then he drank deeply from the cold mountain stream. Even the water tasted different here. No need to bother with buckets and dippers. He tossed a handful of water over his head. Slowly he shook the drops from his eyelids. His brothers, John and James, could tend the farm and measure flour and sugar for the customers in the store. But Sam Houston was not made for that life. It was too tame for the eager young boy. Softly he whistled a call, hoping his friends would hear. His stomach rumbled. He was hungry for some of that stew which Oo-loo-te-ka's wife always served.

He thought briefly about food. His sturdy Scotch-Irish grandfather, Robert Houston, had loved the stew that his wife Margaret had kept at the side of the fireplace. But that was different from this Cherokee dish that Sam loved.

Sam's grandfather had come from Scotland through Londonderry, Ireland, finally to Virginia. His father, Major Samuel Houston, had died when Sam was only about eleven years old. Sam's brave mother, Elizabeth Paxton Houston, had packed up her large family and began the long journey. The major had bought some land in East Tennessee just before his death. The family followed the usual covered-wagon trail across the mountains. Near the Little Hiwassee they settled about ten miles from Maryville, Tennessee.

At first, Sam's mother had put him to work on the farm. However, he didn't become a very good farmer. Then she bought a store in the small town of Maryville. There, with his two older brothers to help him, Sam was put to work running a country store. Again, Sam couldn't keep his mind on the work. At the store he met a few Cherokee traders. They came in to sell the furs that they had trapped. Sam was excited by the stories the Indians told him.

It was not long before Sam put down his feather duster on the counter in the store. He followed his new friends westward to the Indian lands. Here he found a friendship that was deep and lifelong. At first he stayed for only a few days. As time went on, he stayed longer and longer.

This trip he wanted to spend the entire spring and summer with Chief Oo-loo-te-ka's family. The chief liked the daring young white boy. He looked forward to seeing Sam each time.

Suddenly, Sam's ears caught the sound of a twig breaking. Good! He'd surprise them this time. They wouldn't grab him from behind. He slipped behind a tree and waited.

But the surprise was on Sam. John Rogers' arms were around him before he knew what was happening.

"Brother, we've been waiting," the brown boy shouted. He patted Sam on the back as he let him go.

"John, James, it's good to be back!" Sam replied, as he shook hands with both of the boys. A shiver of joy ran down Sam's back. He thought of the good times awaiting them. There would be swimming in the cool streams near the Hiwassee. Then there were the beautiful slender Indian girls who liked to hear him read from the *Iliad.* This was going to be a wonderful summer.

The boys insisted on carrying Sam's shoes for him. The three started running through the woods toward Oo-loo-te-ka's village. Chief John Jolly himself came out to meet them. John Jolly was the American name for Oo-loo-te-ka, which means "He Puts the Drums Away."

"My son, I am glad that you have returned to us," Chief Jolly told Sam. "We were afraid that you might miss the Green Corn Dance this year." When Oo-loo-te-ka had learned that Sam's father was dead, he insisted on adopting Sam into his family.

The Green Corn Dance was one of the most solemn tribal ceremonies. All of the tribe assembled for the fun, and a night of dancing kept the younger members busy. It was only after this special rite in July or August that the women began to pound the corn into meal in stone metates. Sam particularly liked the corn cakes cooked in hot ashes. Some of the corn was parched in the ear. The meal and corn were stored in earthern jars and reed baskets. Sam had no intention of missing this time of fun and frolic. He had managed to get here at just the right time.

Oo-loo-te-ka's home was a large comfortable cabin, capable of holding his entire family plus a guest or two. Behind the cabin were the slave quarters. Chief Jolly had many Negro slaves for whom he had traded furs and baskets of corn. Sam felt completely at home here.

John and James handed Sam some of their clothes as he stripped out of his store-bought things. Without a shirt, he would soon be as brown as they were. They teased him about his pale skin.

One of the girls brought Sam a bowl of stew, which he ate rapidly. He could hardly wait to be off in the woods with the Rogers boys and their friends. As usual there was no talk among the boys. Sam had learned their sign language. The wild animals were not frightened away by the sound of their voices when they signaled to each other.

This special summer remained one of the high spots in Sam Houston's life. He would always remember the feeling of freedom and joy that he felt while he was with these people. But all too soon, though, he began to feel a need to repay their kindness. He slipped away several times to go back to Maryville to borrow money from his family to buy blankets and trinkets for his friends. Sam's mother always used his visits to warn her son that he might someday want something more in life than this freedom he now enjoyed.

As his debts from borrowing mounted, Sam began to know that he must make a way to repay them. It was then that he came home to Maryville with the idea that he could teach school. He had a printer make up a poster that stated that S. Houston would open a school near Maryville. He would teach the three-R's and other special subjects. Actually, Sam had been to school for only a very short time himself. But he had learned much from his reading and his experiences. Indeed, he soon had more students than he could teach.

His school in the log cabin had windows that opened down into the school room and formed desks for the students. It was fine in the warm months, but when the weather began to be cold, Sam had to close his school. He did earn enough to pay his debts. Since his pay was in equal amounts of corn, calico, and money, he had more gifts for his Indian friends.

That winter Sam decided to go back to the Maryville Academy to study more. He had chosen teaching as his career. However, when the professor set him to studying higher math, he quit school. Sam's mind was not geared to math. He would have to find some other way to make a living. But it certainly would not be in the family store or on the farm!

One of Sam's friends, William Willoughby, urged Sam to go with him to watch a recruiting party for the U.S. army. They gazed at the sergeants with their white belts crossed over their chests. The fifes tooted and the drums roared. Sam's chest filled with pride in his country.

"Will, I'm going to do it. I'm going to join the army," he shouted to his friend above the roar of the music. "Will, it's what I want more than anything else."

Will, only fifteen at the time, tried to pull him back, but Sam stepped up to the drumhead and picked up his silver dollar. This act meant that he was enlisting in the army.

An officer spoke to Sam, "Boy, how old are you? Are you sure that you're of age?"

Sam Houston had not even thought about age. He would only be twenty the next day, March 2, 1813. The army would not accept him! His heart sank.

Then the officer spoke again, "If you can get your parents to sign for you, you can join. Your father will have to give his permission."

Sam hesitated a moment before replying, "My father's dead. There's only my mother, and I'm afraid she won't sign for me."

Sam stopped off at the store to tell his brothers first. He thought perhaps they might be able to persuade his mother to sign. But Sam was wrong. His brothers were angry.

"You are entitled to an officer's commission because of our father's part in the Revolution," John Houston told Sam.

"Why do you disgrace the family this way?" James Houston asked. "Wait until you are old enough and then apply for a commission. This is foolish to be just a common soldier!"

Sam answered them briefly, "You will hear from me yet. I'll be a good soldier. Just you wait and see."

Sam's mother was another surprise to him. She perhaps was relieved that his life with the Indians was over. At any rate she signed the document.

"Sam," she said, as she slipped a gold ring on his finger, "the word *Honor* engraved in this ring must always be upheld. Never remove the ring, and never do a dishonorable deed."

She handed Sam the paper. Sam kissed her and left in a hurry to return the paper to the army officer. Life would never again be the same for him.

CHAPTER TWO

Only about a year after he left the home of Oo-loo-te-ka and the peaceful Indian territory, Sam Houston had entered the ranks of the U.S. army. The army life was certainly a change from the freedom of Indian life. His friends, the half-breed brothers, James and John Rogers, also served in the ranks as scouts.

One day the two brothers were lying in the shade of a huge oak tree, talking about their training with the army. They might never have joined up if it hadn't been for Sam. Thus their minds were upon his successes.

"Johnny, our old friend Sam has really gone to the top. It took him only four months to become an officer. He went from sergeant to third lieutenant in that time," James told his brother. "That is really moving; but then we both know what kind of man Sam is. It was easy for him. Much easier than it would be for one of our birth."

James answered, "Do you realize that he's not even twenty-one years old yet?"

"I know," Johnny said, "but he's the kind of man they can never stop. He'll be a general yet. Just you wait and see."

Sam Houston strolled out to the boys under the oak tree just at that time. He shook hands with both of them. Then he dropped to the ground on the grass beside them.

"Sam, is this trouble really going to lead our troops into action?" asked Johnny. He knew about the trouble with Great Britain, but that seemed so far away from them at the moment. What was close to them was the trouble with the Creek Indians.

"You know, Johnny, that Bill Weatherford is determined to drive all the whites out of Alabama. He'll do it anyway he can," answered Sam. Bill Weatherford was a half-breed Creek who hated the white people.

"The Creeks have allied themselves with the British in Canada. There'll certainly be trouble," Sam Houston continued.

"I heard that they had already received arms and ammunition from the British," James added.

"They have. I only pray to God that they'll hold off pushing the whites back," Sam answered, chewing at a blade of grass he had pulled from the earth.

Trouble was not long in coming. On August 30, 1813, Bill Weatherford led a group of Cherokees. They attacked and massacred a settlement of whites at Fort Mims, Alabama. As many as 400 men, women and children were scalped and killed. The nation was shocked at the bloody act. Calls for punishment of the Indians came thick and fast all over the nation.

In Tennessee, General Andrew Jackson had been wounded in a duel just shortly before. However, he rose from his sick bed and began to gather troops. He organized 2,500 volunteers to attack the Creeks. They set out for Alabama. They attacked the Creeks four different times. But the untrained troops found the going rough.

"I knew we would have trouble. Nevertheless, I didn't expect this much fighting from the Indians," Jackson told his officers. "The only way we can make it is to have some well-trained troops to join us."

He sent out a call to the regular army. On February 3, 1814, the 39th Infantry of the U.S. army was sent to join him at Fort Strother. This was the fortress which Jackson and his volunteers had built. It was here for the first time that Sam Houston set eyes on the man who was to become his second foster father. Houston lacked eighteen days of being twenty-one years old. Jackson was forty-six, tall and bony. This was the beginning of a friendship that would last a lifetime.

As the new troops came marching into camp, Jackson was happy.

"This time we'll make it. This is all it takes to make men out of raw recruits. These troops know what training is," Jackson said. He knew that their army discipline would build up the courage of his own ragged volunteers. Sam Houston was proud of the platoon he was given. He had worked them hard. He knew they were fighting men.

"Let's show General Jackson that we are real soldiers," Houston told his men just before they reached Fort Strother. His admiration for the general was great. At last Sam Houston saw his chance to go into actual battle.

The following days at Fort Strother taught Sam Houston a lesson about training troops. That lesson never left him. If a soldier or officer was caught drunk, Jackson had him arrested. In the matter of a man who deserted his post, Jackson ordered the man shot for his actions. Jackson was tough, but fair with his men. They knew the penalty for such actions. Houston was beginning his training for future military leadership.

The next week John and James Rogers reported back to General Jackson from a scouting trip. Their news was exciting to the general and his officers.

"Sir, the Creeks are camped at a place called Tohopeka. It's a sharp bend in the Tallapoosa River near where it joins the Coosa. They call it Horseshoe Bend," John told the general. "They've built a fort of green logs across the mouth of the Bend."

"How many warriors do they have in the party?" asked the general.

"Near as I could tell, Sir, there were about 2,000 men," answered James Rogers. "The area is about 100 acres covered with small timber and brush. I'd say there are about two thousand or more."

"Call the troops, men, and prepare to move on the double to the Tallapoosa," ordered General Jackson.

9

"We can catch them bottled up like that. It may make our task easier."

They marched the short distance of about fifty miles on double quick time. The 39th Infantry of the regular army was also ready for its taste of the fighting.

Jackson had his men surround the Indian fortress. However, before ordering an attack, he gave the Indians time to get their women and children off the battlefield. A few hours later at 12:30 in the afternoon on March 27, 1814, drummers beat the long roll. The battle was on.

Major Lemuel P. Montgomery, for whom the Alabama capital is named, led the charge of Houston's division. Montgomery fell dead as the fort was reached. Houston, just behind him, stepped forward waving his sword. He yelled encouraging words to his platoon to follow him. The battle became thick with arrows, spears, and musket balls flying. The sound of swords and tomahaws filled the air, along with the shouts and yells of the warriors. The wounded covered the ground before the fort.

Houston climbed over the barricade. His men were right behind him, where he was fighting off a ring of Indians with his sword. Despite an arrow buried in his thigh, he kept on his feet and led his men past the barricade. The Creeks dropped back.

There was a short lull in the fighting. At this time, Houston grabbed the arrow and tried to pull it from his leg. When it wouldn't come out, he shouted to a lieutenant nearby.

"Here, Lieutenant, help me get this arrow out. I can't do it by myself," Houston called.

"Sir, I'm afraid it will make the wound bleed too much. You can't stand the loss of blood," the man begged. He gave the arrow a tug and then gave up.

With his eyes blazing, Houston answered, "Pull it out, Sir, and this time you had better succeed, or I'll knock you flat!"

The man gave a second pull on the arrow and out it came. Blood gushed from the wound. Houston shoved his neckerchief into the blood and held it firmly in place. This time he climbed back over the barricade and called for a surgeon. The doctor bound up the wound and stopped the flow of blood.

"Lieutenant, you go back to the camp and rest," said the man with the shock of yellow-white hair. "You're not fit to fight any more today." The man who gave the order was General Jackson.

Despite his deep respect for his commander, Houston was not satisfied with his fighting. He had promised his brothers that he would show them what a good soldier he could be. He didn't mean to be put out of action at the first charge. He would watch for his chance to get back into the fighting.

By night the Creeks had been driven to a remote ravine. They had broken up into small groups. From this gully, they made their last effort. Gunfire and arrows whistled from loopholes in the logs.

From his resting place Houston heard General Jackson call for volunteers to put down this final struggle. In spite of his wounded leg, Houston jumped to his feet. He grabbed the musket of a man in his own platoon and called to all who dared to follow him.

"Come on, those of you who are brave enough! Let's put these Creeks out of business," called the excited Houston. "Let's see what kind of men you are!"

Only a few men trailed along behind him. Most of them were tired of the fight. They wanted to rest a little longer. Without looking back, Houston dashed down the ravine toward the barricade. Only a few yards from the Creeks, Houston felt two rifle balls hit his right arm and shoulder. His arm fell limp at his side. These were the wounds that would trouble him for the rest of his life.

"Come on, you cowards, get after these murderers!" he shouted. His men were not behind him. They did not answer. Houston finally worked his way back to the top of the gully. There he sank to the earth, in pain and unconscious.

"Who is that young officer?" asked General Jackson, who had been watching the fighting from a distance.

"Sir, it's Sam Houston," replied his orderly.

"See that his rank is moved up to that of second lieutenant, at once," ordered General Jackson.

Meanwhile some of the men had succeeded in setting the log barricade on fire. The Indians were forced out of their fortress. They surrendered to Jackson's forces and the battle was over.

Two surgeons worked over Houston. One removed the musket ball from Houston's shoulder. He turned to the other doctor to see how he was doing with the second musket ball.

"I don't see any use in trying to dig this one out," said the second surgeon. "He is almost gone now. He can't live through the night, anyway."

The two men went on to other patients who were in better condition. They did not even cover Houston's body as he lay on the ground in the rain. After all, they had to tend to the living.

The hours went by, with Houston tossing and moaning in pain. When morning finally came, he was still alive. Some of the men made a litter and carried him to Fort Williams about fifty miles away. But when the army moved on, they left him behind as a hopeless case. He had been placed in a small field hospital where he was expected to die at any moment.

Some of the Tennessee volunteers who knew him looked after him. When they finally were ready to leave, they put him on a rough litter between two horses and started on their way to Tennessee. Houston suffered terrible pain during the trip. He screamed when the horses went up or down an incline.

"I just don't see how he keeps on living," said one of the men taking care of him. "His fever has been sky-high most of the time. He's down to skin and bones, but still he goes on living."

To keep the pain down, they gave him doses of whiskey. It seemed a never-ending battle, but the men did not abandon him. Often during the trip he begged them to put him down and leave him. Finally, two months later, Houston, helped by two companions, arrived at his mother's home near Maryville. With his arms around two men, Houston walked up the path to his mother's door. Elizabeth Houston opened the door.

"Don't you know me, Ma?" Houston asked, barely able to speak the words.

Elizabeth stared at him in disbelief. It couldn't be her son. Only his eyes looked like her Sam's. She threw her arms around him and held him close to her.

"My son, my son, you've come home!" she cried.

CHAPTER THREE

By June, 1814, Houston was strong enough to make his way to Knoxville. There he hoped to find a doctor. The only doctor in Knoxville tried to treat him, but gave up. He thought Houston couldn't live.

"Mr. Houston, there's not much I can do for you," the man told him. "Really, I do not think you have long to live."

"Well, when I can get myself on a horse," Houston replied, "I intend to go to Washington. I'll make the army do something for me. They must have something to help my shoulder. This pain is terrible!"

After three months at Knoxville, Houston did make his way to Washington. There he was met with the ruin that had been created by the British in the city. His anger flared up at this sight. Unhappy at the trouble in Washington, Houston returned to Maryville by Christmas.

Elizabeth Houston greeted her son warmly. She hoped that at long last he would be ready to settle down.

"Son," she pleaded with her son, "we need you in the store. Or at least to help out on the farm. There is room for all of us here."

"Mother, my dear, I do not intend to spend my life keeping a store or teaching school. I want more from life than that," Houston replied gently.

"But you're not well, and anything else will be too hard for you," Elizabeth argued. She did not want to see Sam leave home again.

"Then I'll apply for my rating in the regular army,"

he told his mother. "The 39th Infantry is no more, but surely they'll have something for me."

Houston was finally offered a place as a second lieutenant in the 1st Infantry. It was stationed in New Orleans at that time. He went to Nashville to equip himself. There he met a friend, Edward Douglas White. Together they took a flatboat to Natchez, Mississippi. From Natchez they boarded a paddle-wheeled steamer for New Orleans.

Soon after Houston's arrival in New Orleans, the army doctors decided that the musket ball must be removed from his shoulder. Otherwise he might lose his arm. A surgeon located the bullet, and Houston was given a swig of strong whiskey. He braced himself over the back of a chair. The doctor dug into his shoulder to remove the ball. Houston got through the operation, but the pain and bleeding left him weak and dizzy.

All winter long he lay in his bed trying to recover. But all the rest was not enough. The army could not give him a satisfactory rating. They ordered him to go to New York for more treatment. Finally he was allowed to go home on a visit.

After Christmas on January 1, 1817, the army ordered him to report for duty in Nashville. Within three months he was made a first lieutenant. However, the most important thing about being in Nashville was that Andrew Jackson was in charge of the Southern Division.

"Sam, my boy, it's been a long time since Horseshoe Bend," the white-haired man said as he shook hands with Houston. "We have much to talk about."

"Sir, it's good to see you again," Sam told General Jackson. "I would like to hear you tell about New Orleans. That must have been a real fight. I'm sorry I missed it."

"Indeed it was," replied Jackson. "We even had the pirate, Jean Lafitte, on our side. Why, one time when we met in front of a church there in New Orleans — " the General let his mind go back to the days with his soldiers in the old city. The two men sat and talked for hours about the battles in which they had fought.

Then Houston brought up a subject nearer to his heart, the Cherokees. Despite the troubles with the tribes, he always had a soft spot in his heart for the people of Oo-loo-te-ka.

"Sam, my sources in Washington say that you are the only man who has real influence with the Cherokees," Jackson told Houston. "They say that you can stop a new outbreak of trouble."

"They are my people," Sam said. "I lived among the tribe of Oo-loo-te-ka in Tennessee. I don't know whether I can be of any help or not, but I certainly would like to try. I don't like seeing them pushed further west unless they want to go."

"Would you consider a job as subagent to the Cherokees?" Jackson asked.

"Sir, I'm afraid that the Indians have been cheated by the agents. They won't be happy to see me as an agent," Sam answered.

"Whatever we do, Sam, the government intends to enforce the treaty. They shall be moved west of the Mississippi, in spite of anything we can do," Jackson told him.

"It seems there is nothing else to do. I don't want them hurt any more," Sam said, running his hands through his brown hair. "Yes, I'll do it. You go ahead and start working on the appointment."

Sam put on his Indian clothes and set out to join Chief Jolly's people. His adopted father joyfully welcomed him back into the tribe. He had many things that he wanted to talk over with his adopted son.

"My son, you know that my tribe fears the land west of the Mississippi. It is the home of the Black Evil, of death and misery. We were born to live in the Sun Land, our true home," the old man sadly told Sam. "Our gods are here. It will mean trouble and sorrow for us to leave our homes."

All the young braves gathered around to hear what

their white brother had to say. They listened intently to his words.

"Without allies, you will be weak," Sam told the chief and the young braves. They knew at once that Houston was right. There was no chance of the Five Nations uniting.

Oo-loo-te-ka turned to his braves. He spoke slowly, "My adopted son has always walked straight with us. He understands us better than any other white man. It is time that we follow what he tells us to do. We will accept the new lands. We will not make trouble."

At once the tribe began to get ready to leave. The government furnished the 109 braves with good rifles. They were given flatboats with supplies for all their needs to carry with them to their new homes.

However, Houston did not go with the tribe to Arkansas. Just as they were ready to leave, Oo-loo-te-ka's aged brother, Chief Tallontuske, came to Knoxville with a group of his people. They had already moved to the land west of the Mississippi. Now Tallontuske was on his way to Washington to ask for freedom for his people. The governor of Tennessee asked Houston to put on his Indian clothes and go with the Indians.

It was February 5, 1818, when Secretary of War Calhoun welcomed the group. The tall man with thick greyish hair spoke in a dry voice.

"It is a pleasure to welcome you to Washington," he said, holding out his hand to the chief. "I want you to know that you will have fair treatment from our president."

Chief Tallontuske bowed deeply upon hearing Calhoun's words. He did not comment upon the fairness. After a few more words, the delegation turned to file out the door.

"Houston," Calhoun called, "I want to speak to you!"

Houston turned and waited until Calhoun reached the door. He expected to be thanked by the secretary of war for his efforts to smooth over a bad time with the Indians. Instead Calhoun spoke to him in anger.

"Why have you insulted your government by appearing here in such outlandish garb?" Calhoun demanded to know.

"Sir, I felt it would be best to dress like the people that I am with. They will be more likely to listen to me if they think I am one of them," Houston answered.

He was shocked by Calhoun's attitude. Moreover, Houston was a United States Indian subagent. As such he was wearing the clothes suited to his job.

"Mr. Houston, you should know better. Before you take these people in to see the president, put on civilized dress!" Calhoun ordered. Houston bowed low, turned upon his heel, and walked out of the room without an answer to the demand.

The whole affair was disgusting to Houston. The Indians were bribed to return to Arkansas and keep their peace. Chief Tallontuske received a sum of one thousand dollars. The others received five hundred dollars. Houston's anger toward Calhoun was to continue for many years to come. On March 1, 1818, Houston resigned from the army.

Without his army pay, Houston found himself in debt. He returned to Tennessee, where he met Judge James Trimble. Trimble became interested in Houston and offered to teach him law.

"Sam, I am sure that you can complete the course of study in a year and a half," Trimble told him. He knew that Houston was smart, but he did not know how fast Houston would work. In only six months, Houston was ready for his bar examination.

"Sir, I can never thank you enough for all your help and encouragement," Sam told Judge Trimble. "I think now I have my life straightened out. I know what I want to do."

He certainly did know. Soon Houston became district attorney in Nashville. When that did not bring in enough money, Houston resigned. He went into private practice where he made money rapidly. Soon he was elected to Congress. By 1827 he became governor of Tennessee.

As head of the state of Tennessee, Houston found himself the most eligible young bachelor in Nashville. He said many times that he did not intend to court any young woman until he could offer her the kind of life she should have. But then he became friendly with the family of John Allen of Gallatin, Tennessee. He visited the home on the Cumberland often when the horses were racing.

Allen's daughter, Eliza, was only fourteen when Houston first saw her. He paid little attention to her. But after he became governor, Eliza was sixteen and very attractive. Houston fell in love with the young beauty. She was tiny, fair with blond hair and blue eyes. Houston made up his mind quickly.

"Eliza, my dear, I know that you are very young, but I just can't live without you," Houston told the girl. "I want you to marry me and come to live with me in Nashville. I will make a good life for you there."

"Sam, I don't know. I wonder what Father will say?" Eliza answered.

"I'll ask him for your hand at once," Sam almost shouted, so pleased at her seeming agreement.

What Sam Houston did not know was that Eliza had already fallen in love with young Will Tyree. Will was ill with tuberculosis. At the time he was away in Cuba trying to overcome his illness. Eliza could not consider marrying a man with T.B. Well-bred young women just didn't do things like that.

"Eliza," John Allen told his young daughter, "forget the past. You are young. This is a chance for you to become the first lady of a great state." Her father urged her to accept Houston's proposal. Her mother also favored the match.

"But, Papa, I love Will Tyree," Eliza objected.

Her mother interrupted her, "Eliza, dear, no good can ever come of that love. You must think of your future."

It was easy for the parents to tell the young girl that

she must take Houston as her husband. The engagement was announced just before Christmas in 1828.

Shortly after the announcement, sad news came to Nashville. Andrew Jackson's wife, Rachel, had died. She was buried on Christmas Eve in the garden of the Hermitage, Jackson's home.

Later Sam sat with Jackson in the parlor at the Hermitage. They spoke of Rachel and what her loss meant to Old Hickory.

"Sam, I just don't think I can go on without her," Jackson told Houston. "Life doesn't seem to have any meaning now."

"But, Sir, the nation needs you. There is much for you to do," Sam tried to comfort the saddened man as he spoke.

"Well, enough of my sorrow, Sam," Jackson told Sam. "We must talk of your plans for the future. Young Eliza is a lovely girl. She will be an asset to you in your political career."

The wedding took place at Gallatin on January 22, 1829, but in her room before the ceremony the young bride-to-be wept.

"Eliza, you must not cry. Your eyes will be all red. After all, you may someday be the wife of a president of the United States. This man is a friend of Andrew Jackson. Surely, Sam Houston may follow in Jackson's footsteps," her mother told her. She handed Eliza her handkerchief as she continued arranging her veil.

Eliza's father came to get her. She held tightly to his arm as he led her down the stairs. Houston was waiting in the elegant drawing room of the Allen home. Most of Tennessee society was there to witness the wedding of its governor. After a gala reception, the bride and groom spent the night at the Allen home. The next morning, in spite of a light snowstorm, the young couple mounted horses and rode toward Nashville.

On the way to Nashville they visited in the homes of friends for several days. Once in Nashville they moved into a suite at the local inn. Nashville society welcomed them warmly. They seemed to be the ideal young couple. The next three months, however, brought a change in the marriage. No one knew what happened. Houston and Eliza refused to talk about it. But on the night of April 11, 1829, Houston returned from a political debate. Supposedly, he found Eliza crying over some old letters which she was burning. A quarrel resulted. Houston told Eliza that she should not stay if she didn't want to. Whether it was her old love affair or Houston's jealousy, the world will never know. The storm broke over Nashville on April 16.

At the Nashville Inn a clerk asked a visitor, "Have you heard about Houston and his wife?"

"What about them?"

"The governor and his wife have separated. She has gone home to her father's house," said the clerk.

Houston was not at home when his wife left. When he discovered that she was gone, he rode his mare wildly to the Allen home. He was allowed to see Eliza only with his wife's aunt present.

"Eliza, please forgive me," Houston begged his wife.

"I'm sorry, Sam, but I cannot live with you anymore," Eliza told him with tears in her eyes. "I just can't do it."

"But, Eliza, I'll try to be a better husband to you," Sam said. "Please come home with me."

"Sam, things cannot change between us. It's over for us," Eliza answered.

When Houston returned to Nashville, he wrote to Mr. Allen. Houston spoke of his unhappiness about the affair. He said that he hoped Mr. Allen could get Eliza to return to Nashville. He would do anything to regain Eliza's love.

All kinds of charges were made against Houston in Nashville. He stayed alone in his rooms. His friends came to call on him, but he would not go out. They told him about the gossip that was raging all over town. But Houston would not defend himself.

He waited in vain for an answer to his letter to Mr. Allen. None came. Then he wrote a letter to the Speaker of the Tennessee Senate. He was giving up his position as governor. Houston felt that these were the darkest hours in his life. In the time that he remained in his rooms, he thought of his days among the Cherokee people. He had not seen his foster father in eleven years. He needed the peace and quiet of the Cherokees. Houston made up his mind to leave Nashville.

One week after he gave up his office, Houston boarded the steam packet, *Red Rover*. He had booked passage under an assumed name. Two of his friends went with him to the wharf. Houston wore an Indian blanket over old clothes. On the boat he met a light-hearted Irishman named Haralson. Together they bought a flatboat at Cairo, Illinois. They loaded it with provisions, took aboard a handy man, a Negro boy, and a dog. Once again Houston was on his way to his foster father's home.

CHAPTER FOUR

The men on the flatboat worked the craft across the Mississippi. They were about halfway between Memphis and Helena, Arkansas. After crossing the strong current of the river, they drifted slowly along the bank, enjoying the bright spring days. Houston was not quite at ease yet. He consumed large amounts of whiskey that they bought from traders along the river. At Helena, they went into the leading saloon. While they were there, a huge figure darkened the door. Haralson excitedly introduced Houston to the newcomer.

"Sam, this is Jim Bowie. He and his brother own a cotton plantation and a sawmill in Louisiana," Haralson said.

Sam put out his hand, a little groggily. He had heard of Jim Bowie before. He was pleased to see the man. However, he knew that his own looks were rather bad. Maybe Bowie would shun him.

"This is Sam Houston? The governor of Tennessee?" Jim Bowie spoke without belief. It was hard for him to realize that this dirty drunken figure could be the great Sam Houston!

Bowie grabbed Houston's hand and shook it mightily. "What are you doing here in Arkansas?" he asked.

Sam answered, "I'm on my way to Indian territory. I want to spend some time with my friends, the Cherokees." He really didn't want to talk too much about himself. In fact, his plans were not quite clear to himself yet.

"How have you been, Jim?" asked Haralson. "I heard that you have been in Texas several times."

A YOUNG SAM HOUSTON...from an early print.

"That I have, indeed," answered Bowie. "In fact, I've been thinking of settling down there. It's might pretty country."

"What about the land? Is it cheap?" asked Houston. "Can Americans get a good deal from the Mexicans?" Texas had been on his mind for some time now. He had an urge to go exploring the wild new country.

"It's wide open right now, Sam, but I have a feeling it won't last. The Mexicans are going to be a little more careful about letting too many Americans settle there," Bowie answered, sipping on a large mug of ale.

"Is there any chance of its becoming a part of the United States?" Houston asked, pulling out his knife and starting to whittle.

"Not a chance, Sam. They aren't going to let something that good go without a fight," Bowie answered. "Right now, you have to be a Catholic even to buy land. They will certainly limit the number of foreigners they let in."

The men chatted for some time about affairs in the United States. Bowie asked about Andrew Jackson. Bowie had known the general at the Battle of New Orleans. There was much to talk about. The session lasted until early morning hours before Houston and Haralson pulled out. They would continue down the Mississippi until they reached the Arkansas. The next big stop would be Little Rock.

At Little Rock, Houston wrote to Andrew Jackson, telling him about his unhappy marriage. He said that he was without a doubt the most miserable man in the world. Then he told Jackson that he was on his way to see Oo-loo-te-ka's family. In two hours' time he and Haralson would board a steamer to go to Oo-loo-te-ka's wigwam.

Houston, Haralson, and a new companion, John Litton, boarded the steamer, *Facility*. This boat would take them as far as Fort Gibson, the nearest military post to the Cherokee village. Oo-loo-te-ka heard that Houston was on board the *Facility.* It was night when the steamer arrived at the boat landing. Black slaves belonging to Oo-loo-te-ka brought torches to light the way. Houston and his companions had drunk so much whiskey that they had to be helped off the boat. But the old chief threw his arms around Houston. He was delighted to see his foster son again.

"My son, we are glad to have you back," Oo-loo-te-ka said as he hugged Houston again and again. "We have needed your help very much. We want you to talk with the Great White Father in Washington."

Houston was led to the chief's large comfortable wigwam. Ten or twelve slaves took care of Oo-loo-te-ka's family. The wigwam was really a large plantation in a grove of sycamores and cottonwoods. The old chief owned over five hundred head of cattle. Oo-loo-te-ka provided well for his guests who were always welcome. He killed at least one beef a week for his family and guests. Houston felt like a weary wanderer returned at last to his father's house.

Oo-loo-te-ka had ordered a party to honor Houston's return. His old friends, John and James Rogers, and their recently widowed sister, Diana Rogers Gentry, were there. Diana, or Tiana, as the family called her, was to be of great comfort to Houston. With her love and kindness he would try to make sense out of the wreck of his life.

"My son, I want you to help us at a meeting of the Grand Council," Oo-loo-te-ka said to Houston. "We need your advice. The agents and traders have been cheating us. They pay us only with paper money. Then when we try to buy goods, they charge us too much."

Oo-loo-te-ka knew that the traders were making huge profits. The Indians did not know the value of the paper money. He felt that Houston could help the Indians.

Houston remained drunk for the best part of every day. Because of his drinking, the Indians gave him the nickname, "The Big Drunk." It was a name that would follow Houston even after he recovered from his terrible sorrow. But he remained sober when the need arose. Houston spent much time in traveling among the Indian tribes. He sought to help them with their problems with the agents.

After a serious illness, probably malaria, Houston wrote a long letter to Andrew Jackson. He told Jackson of his efforts to improve the conditions of the Indians. Among other things he mentioned that he was thinking of taking up his political career. However, that was not to come for a long time. He really tried to make himself a part of the Indian life.

During the first summer at Oo-loo-te-ka's, Houston applied for admission to the Cherokee tribe. In October he received his certificate.

"My brother," said the chief who presented the document, "this paper is given because of your past service to our nation. We trust your efforts to help us. You have been a good and true friend to the Cherokees."

Thinking of himself as a Cherokee now, Houston had plaited his hair in a long queue. He dressed himself according to the customs of his people. He wore a white doeskin shirt worked with beads, yellow leather leggings, a headdress of eagle feathers. Sometimes he wore a turban of figured silk. When it became cool weather, he wore a bright blanket over his outfit.

The next spring Houston made a trip to Washington. He was a member of a Cherokee group. Their purpose was to complain about the bad Indian agents. In his bright buckskins and blanket, Houston was received at the president's house. Since Jackson was president, Houston was given a hearty welcome. His clothing made no difference to this president. They were good friends.

On the way home through Tennessee, small crowds greeted Houston. They were showing their faith in him. But he also met political enemies who did not make him so welcome. It was probably this trip that made Houston realize that his Indian life would not last. But he tried to keep his pleasant way of life.

Houston was still legally married to Eliza. However, as a citizen of the Cherokee nation, other laws applied. When a brave and his squaw decided that they could no longer live together, they "split the blanket." Oo-loo-te-ka told him that since he and Eliza had separated, they were no longer married. This made the way clear for Houston to court and marry the beautiful Tiana, a widow.

Tiana had nursed Houston back from his bout with malaria in 1829. Her dead husband, David Gentry, had been a white blacksmith who was well respected by the Indians. Tiana was related to most of the important Cherokee families in Arkansas. She was described as tall, willowy, and handsome.

Houston and Tiana were married by Cherokee custom. Houston built a log house near the Neosho River. It was in an apple orchard about thirty miles from the chief's lodge. Houston called this new home, "Wigwam Neosho."

Sometime after his marriage, Houston opened a trader's store. He ordered his goods from Nashville. He promised to provide supplies for the Indians at honest prices. He sold such things as kettles, blankets, rope, bridles, flour, and soap. Among the other things Houston ordered were nine barrels of liquor.

Houston went to Fort Gibson to get his supplies. When he wanted to take the liquor, the commander at the fort objected.

"Houston, it's against the law for a white man to take supplies of liquor into the Indian nation," said Colonel Matthew Arbuckle.

"I am a member of the Cherokee nation now," answered Houston sharply. "It is within my right to take anything I want."

"That does not change the fact that you are a white man," argued Arbuckle. The quarrel was finally referred to Washington. Houston was given permission to take the liquor into his own home for personal use. Unfortunately, it seemed that Houston then devoted himself to consuming all of his huge liquor store. He seemed a poor risk ever to pick himself up. But this man was Sam Houston. He could overcome this weakness!

One morning Houston was slumped under a tree in front of his log home, sleeping off a drunken stupor. Tiana came running from the store to awaken him.

"Sam, Sam! There is a man here with a message from your brother. Your mother is ill," Tiana said breathlessly. "She is not expected to live. They want you to come." She knew what this message would do to her man. He would be torn apart because his mother was so important to him.

Houston shook himself awake. He dressed and hurried to Fort Gibson to take a steamer to his home. He might just get there in time. He did, and Elizabeth Houston gave him her blessing shortly before she died. Somehow her death changed Houston. He went back to Arkansas, but he was a different man. He was no longer content to remain in the peaceful, easy-going life of the Cherokees.

A message came from John Wharton, a friend in Nashville. John was the younger brother of William Wharton, who had gone to Texas and married the daughter of Jared Ellison Groce, a wealthy plantation owner.

"I have heard of your intended expedition against Texas," wrote John Wharton. "I suppose, if it is true, you will let those of us in Nashville know about it."

When Houston did not answer Wharton's question, Wharton went on to New Orleans and set up a law practice. From there he visited Texas. He liked it so much that he was preparing to move to Texas. He wrote to Houston again.

"I think you should visit Texas. It is a fine place. You can get a grant of land and be near your friends. Who knows what time may bring about?" Wharton wrote in his letter.

What Wharton did not know was that Houston needed money in order to move on with his life. Houston set out for New York by way of New Orleans. There he met a businessman, James Prentiss. Prentiss agreed to lend him money for a survey trip to Texas.

From New York, Houston went to Washington to visit Andrew Jackson. Earlier he had promised Jackson that he would not make an unlawful filibuster into Texas. He renewed this promise now. Then the talk took on a new turn.

"Sam, you have heard the talk about John Eaton? The papers are saying that he was removed from office because of you," Jackson told Houston. "They are saying that he tried to give you a fraudulent contract for Indian rations."

"General, you know that isn't so!" Houston replied. "William Stanberry is just trying to hurt your administration."

"I know the truth of the situation, Sam," Jackson answered. "Peggy Eaton has not been received by Washington ladies. It's not fair, Sam, the way they are treating her. Stanberry is just trying to use the situation to hurt us."

"Mrs. Calhoun is at the bottom of this whole thing," Houston told Jackson. "She refuses to speak to Mrs. Eaton. She thinks Peggy is not good enough for her. Then Eaton resigned because of the situation?"

"Yes, that was the reason he gave me," Jackson replied.

The next day Houston sent Stanberry a note questioning Stanberry's remarks in the paper. Stanberry refused to answer. Houston was furious. He told his friends that he intended to punish Stanberry for the insult. From that time on Houston carried a heavy walking stick.

One evening Houston and two of his friends saw Stanberry crossing to their side of the street.

"Are you Mr. Stanberry?" asked Houston.

Stanberry replied shortly, "I am."

Houston exclaimed, "Then you are a rascal!" He raised the stick and started for Stanberry.

"Oh, no, don't!" cried Stanberry, starting to run.

Houston tried to hold the man, but his injured shoulder wouldn't let him hold Stanberry. Stanberry's hat fell to the ground. As he bent to pick it up, he tripped and fell. He started yelling and raised his feet to protect himself. Houston began hitting him with the hickory cane. When he was satisfied that he had punished him enough, Houston stopped. Stanberry stumbled to his feet and ran away.

Although it was an illegal move, the House of Representatives called for Houston's arrest and punishment. Houston was given forty-eight hours to prepare his defense. He came to the bar of the House with his attorney, Francis Scott Key, the author of *The Star Spangled Banner*. Key did such a poor job that Houston ended by presenting his own defense. Houston's speech was so moving that the actor Junius Brutus Booth complimented him highly.

Houston was found "guilty as charged." He was sentenced to be reprimanded by the Speaker of the House. The Speaker carried out his sentence. However, he spent a long time in complimenting Houston upon his character and intelligence. He ended his speech with a mild statement, "I do reprimand you accordingly."

Finally, Houston was charged in the District Court of Columbia with criminal assault. This was what should have been done in the first place. Houston was convicted this time and fined $500 and costs. Andrew Jackson later dropped the sentence, saying that it was too much.

This event was a major turning point in Houston's life. Out of all the trials and hearings, Houston became a national figure, popular with the people. Without this trouble, he might have remained unknown to most of the nation.

All the time the trials were going on, Houston was working on his plans to go to Texas. The man in New York failed to help him with money. Andrew Jackson came to his aid with some money. On August 16, Houston received a passport which gave him free passage through Indian country.

When he set out for Texas, he first went by Wigwam Neosho. He had made up his mind to settle his domestic affairs. Tiana understood that she could not go back with him to his white life. However, it was understood that a Cherokee wife of a white man should be cared for well. Houston gave her all of the Neosho property with its fields and two slaves. He left Neosho riding a bob-tailed mule named "Jack." He later traded "Jack" for a better-looking horse. After a ride of some twelve hundred miles, Houston discovered that Texas needed him as much as he needed Texas!

CHAPTER FIVE

After shopping briefly at Nacogdoches, Texas, Houston made his way directly to San Felipe de Austin, the colony which Stephen F. Austin had established. Usually in Texas men traveled together for protection. However, Houston, used to traveling alone, found his own way along the Camino Real. San Felipe was a village of some thirty families, its raw, crude buildings gleaming in the winter sun.

Houston went at once to the home of Stephen Austin. There he discovered that Austin was not at home. However, on the steps of the house, he met a friend from the past, Jim Bowie. Together they hunted out the nearest saloon. Over mugs of ale, they talked about Texas.

"Jim, I intend to apply for a land grant here," Houston told his friend Bowie. "I want to make Texas my home from now on."

"It's a good land," Bowie answered. "I have already staked my claim here. I married Ursula Veramendi, the daughter of the vice-governor of Coahuila-Texas. We have two children, and I have bought about 750 thousand acres of land. I couldn't ask for anything better."

"You are to be congratulated, Bowie," Houston said. "Your future must be assured. I hope I can succeed as well as you have." He was indeed hopeful after hearing Bowie's story.

"Sam, there are other things we need to talk about," Jim proceeded to say. "You know, I mentioned before that the Mexicans will not allow any more American settlers into the state. But by bribes, immigrants are arriving every day from the United States. I feel sure that a fight will be brewing if things continue."

"I am sure you are right. I am staying at the Virginia House. I heard there that a meeting has been called for April 1," said Houston, sipping from his mug. "Since Mexico has rid itself of Spain, things are likely to come to a head."

"We want a separate state from Coahuila. This Santa Anna has imposed laws we cannot live with," Bowie told his drinking companion. "I'm not even sure that a separate state will be enough to satisfy most settlers."

"Well, there's one thing I can do," said Sam. "I can get the Indians to be on our side if trouble comes."

"Why don't you come along with me to San Antonio? That's the place to talk with many of the Indians. They come here to trade. You can stay with my father-in-law's family," Bowie offered. "They will welcome a visitor."

Houston did travel to San Antonio. There he talked with several of the Indian tribes. He made an agreement for some of the chiefs to go to Fort Gibson. There they could talk to the American officials.

After a visit with Bowie's family, he went back to San Felipe to visit Stephen Austin. Austin was rather suspicious of newcomers. Nevertheless, he entertained Houston during his visit.

"Houston, I came here to make this my home," Austin said. "I intend to become a good Mexican citizen. I will do everything required of me. I do not intend to join the group that want war with Mexico."

"Mr. Austin, I intend to become a citizen of Texas, too. I'm afraid the rush of immigrants may cause trouble for those of us who want peace," Houston told him. Now Houston could see that Wharton's ideas could cause much trouble for peace-loving settlers.

Houston told Austin of his desire to purchase a land grant. Austin arranged the purchase. Houston bought about four thousand acres on Karankawa Bay. By this purchase on December 24, 1832, Houston became a Texas landowner.

From San Felipe Houston went back to Nacogdoches. While there his new friends asked him to run as a delegate to the convention at San Felipe. Houston consented to enter the race. Then he left for Louisiana. He had written to Andrew Jackson a letter he did not want to trust to Mexican mails. He reported that the Texans wanted a separate state government. Unless order was restored, they would break away from Mexico. If the Texans could not borrow money from the United States, they might appeal to England.

Houston then returned to Nacogdoches. There he found that he had been elected as a delegate. William Wharton was to be chairman. At San Felipe Houston was made chairman of a committee to draft a state constitution. Stephen F. Austin was appointed ambassador to the Mexican government of Santa Anna.

After the convention Houston returned to Nacogdoches. There he made many new friends, among them Adolphus Sterne and Henry Raguet. Adolphus and Eva Sterne invited Houston to move into their comfortable home. Houston accepted eagerly. Very soon at a party given by the Sternes, Houston was introduced to the beautiful Anna Raguet, the teen-aged daughter of Henry Raguet. She was the most attractive young belle of Nacogdoches.

"Sam, I tell you, she's just right for you," Eva Sterne told Houston. "She's intelligent, beautiful, and rich. How could a man do better? Eva was eager to make a match for their well-liked guest.

"But, Eva, you know that I am still legally married in Tennessee. I can't think about marriage or courtship under the circumstances," Sam answered sadly. He knew that he was in his forties. Anna was still just a teen-ager. This match would be impossible for him. Still he was attracted to Anna. This was one friendship that would last for Houston. Even after Anna married another man, they were still friends.

Adolphus Sterne interrupted his friend's conversation with Eva. "You know, Sam, Texas is going to be different from now on. Wharton and his bunch are determined to free Texas from Mexico. We have many noisy, second-rate people here who will certainly get us into trouble."

"You're right, Adolphus, we're headed for trouble," Sam answered slowly.

Sterne continued, "I just had a report that about 2,000 immigrants have landed at the mouth of the Brazos in the last two months."

"Well, for my own part, I intend to follow a middle-of-the stream course. I don't think it will do any good to take sides with either group. Stephen Austin is content to remain under Santa Anna's rule. I'm afraid of either course of action."

Shortly after this conversation, news came of Stephen Austin's arrest in Saltillo. He was taken to Mexico City where he remained in custody until 1835. The revolutionists in Texas were sure that Texas would now seek to free itself from Mexico.

Sam Houston, after thinking about the talk with Eva Sterne, decided to improve his future prospects. First of all, he applied for a divorce from Eliza. This would free him to marry Anna Raguet, should she decide to marry him. Also, he wanted to make his Texas citizenship firmer. He allowed himself to be baptized into the Catholic faith. Eva Sterne was his godmother for the ceremony. Now he could freely pursue his course as a politician and lawyer in his new home.

Santa Anna had himself made president of the Mexican Republic. Then he did away with the state legislatures and named his own governors. Most of the states gave in easily to the change, but not Zacatecas. They rebelled, and Santa Anna promptly crushed them. He ordered punishment for the rebels. He suspected that the

Texans would not bow down to his changes either. He would have to drive the invaders back into the United States. Fearing capture and punishment, the Texans living in Monclova fled back into Texas.

Andrew Briscoe, a merchant at Anahuac, expressed his feelings over the situation. He was arrested by Captain Antonio Tenorio and tossed into jail. The citizens of San Felipe captured a messenger from whom they learned of Santa Anna's plan for Texas.

A group of two hundred angry men met at San Felipe. Twenty-five young daredevils decided to go to Anahuac and settle with Captain Tenorio at once. William Barret Travis, a young Georgia lawyer, was picked as their leader. The action they took was short and sweet. They seized the sloop *Ohio* and loaded it with a small cannon and some powder with one cannon ball. When they reached Anahuac, they fired the one shot. It hit the fort, raised some dust, but did little damage.

Travis boldly demanded Tenorio's surrender. Tenorio along with fifty men surrendered. They pledged never to fight against Texas. Then Travis paroled them with arms to protect themselves against the Indians. They were to march to San Antonio.

War fever had seized the Texans. In Nacogdoches Houston was named commander-in-chief of East Texas. There was no army, but Houston at once issued a call to all counties to organize a militia.

"All troops should bring their own arms and ammunition when they volunteer," Houston announced. "I want the men of Texas to have their arms in order. To have liberty, we must be watchful!"

The troops eagerly flocked to Gonzales. They called themselves the "Volunteer Army of Texas." They sent word to San Felipe that they were ready to fight. Stephen Austin had been released in the summer. He told the delegates to the Consultation that he would lead the new army. He left twenty delegates in San Felipe to carry on until all of the delegates arrived. He proceeded to go with the troops.

Meanwhile, Sam Houston arrived in San Felipe. He decided to follow Austin. He would bring back enough delegates to carry on business. Houston was back in San Felipe in a few days with the needed delegates. They drew up a plan for a temporary government. Henry Smith was chosen governor; James Robinson, lieutenant governor; and Houston was given the job as major general of the army.

Houston's first order was sent to James W. Fannin. Fannin was stationed at the gates to San Antonio. Houston wanted him to pull back to Goliad and Gonzales for the time being. When they had enough equipment, then they could march on San Antonio.

"I don't think anything can be gained without enough arms and ammunition," Houston said. "We'll have to pull back."

"But, Sam, retreat is cowardly," Wyatt Hanks told him. "They'll run when they see our men advancing! They're really cowards at heart." Hanks was loud in his criticism of Houston.

Houston had to endure the many charges hurled at him. Proper respect for the military chain of command was lacking. Houston did his best to organize a proper headquarters at San Felipe. Communication was bad. Houston's few orders were not obeyed promptly.

Finally, a group of volunteers led by Ben Milam tired of the waiting. They stormed San Antonio on December 5, 1835. Milam was killed in the fight, but after five days, General Cos surrendered. He pledged not to fight in Texas again. He along with his 1,400 men were sent back to their homes in Mexico.

Once again the cries against Houston's leadership broke out. The success of the San Antonio campaign convinced many Texans that Houston was wrong in holding back.

"I tell you, men, for once and for all, this Houston

has to be replaced," shouted Dr. James Grant. Grant wanted to pursue the Mexicans into their homeland. He wanted to march at once to Matamoros and take the city. "We'll teach these scoundrels a lesson they won't forget!"

When Houston learned of Grant's plan, he disagreed. However, he ordered Jim Bowie to take over command. Bowie didn't get Houston's orders. When he failed to march, the General Council at San Felipe ordered Frank Johnson to take the expedition to Matamoros. Johnson refused the job, and Fannin was ordered to take over. In the meantime Johnson decided to take the job. This made two commanders for the expedition.

After Bowie's failure to take the group to Matamoros, Houston ordered him to San Antonio.

"Jim, this action must be taken at once. We must demolish the Alamo, remove all the cannon and munitions, and abandon the place. We cannot defend it at present," Houston told Jim Bowie. He knew that the rage brought on by the Matamoros expedition would make it necessary for him to stay in San Felipe. He felt that Dr. Grant had risked the whole Texan cause for his own personal gain.

In the meantime a group of ill-fated men were gathering at the Alamo in San Antonio. Bowie had not obeyed Houston's orders. He was at the Alamo along with David Crockett, William B. Travis, and about two hundred others. The Mexicans were surrounding the outer walls. The most terrible siege of American history was about to begin. When Bowie took pneumonia and typhoid fever, Travis assumed command of the men. A message was sent out by Travis declaring that this fight would end in victory or death.

Along with Travis' message of proud despair from the Alamo arrived the news that Johnson and his troops had been wiped out near San Patricio, one hundred miles north of Matamoros.

Suddenly Houston's popularity was on the rise. He

was needed by Texas once more. Everywhere people were talking about the desperate state of the Texans at the Alamo.

"There is only one hope of relieving them," Houston told Governor Smith. "James Fannin has 450 men at Goliad. They can be sent to the Alamo at once."

Fannin failed to follow Houston's orders. He said that the roads were too muddy for his supply wagons. Although thirty-two men from Gonzales reached San Antonio, it was false hope. Five days later the last of the Alamo's heroes was dead. What remained was the cry that was to follow the Texans through the rest of the struggle, "Remember the Alamo!"

With this sad defeat Houston sent word to Fannin to blow up the defenses at Goliad and to join him. But Fannin did not act right away. He was captured and all of his command were slain. Houston, in Gonzales at the time, started his long retreat.

Although he did not discuss it with anyone, Houston had planned his strategy well. He knew that the deeper he led the Mexicans into Texas, the harder it would be for them to supply their forces with food and ammunition. Also, it would be more difficult to keep in touch with the Mexican government. Actually, all the Texans really stood to lose was land, and there was plenty of that. Houston knew he could retreat until he was in a better position to fight. Then he would strike!

But his enemies were arguing that retreat was not the way wars were won. Houston was mad, they said. There was panic everywhere. People were in the headlong flight back toward the Sabine River. Families packed up and fled. Some had only boys and old men to help them. Their shoes wore out, and they walked barefoot through the Texas mud. It was cold weather this March. Wagons bogged down in the mud or at the rivers. This was the great Runaway Scrape. Even the government was on the run, including David G. Burnet, who had been elected president of the new provisional government.

The public continued to press Houston to stand and fight. Burnet wrote to Houston about the retreat. "People are laughing you to shame!" Burnet declared. Even Santa Anna was sure that the war was over. He divided his army to make easier the mopping up operations. His officers protested the move, but Santa Anna was confident.

At one place where Houston's army camped, he had two graves dug. He hung a sign over the graves. One was for the first man who tried to get the men to mutiny. The other was for any one who dared to volunteer. Houston was determined to keep his army together.

Finally Houston's forces reached a fork in the road. They could go toward the Sabine and the U.S., or they could take the road to Harrisburg. Houston said nothing. He chose the Harrisburg fork. By April 18th the army was on Buffalo Bayou across from the burned remains of Harrisburg. Santa Anna had burned the village. He was pursuing the fleeing government of David Burnet.

Houston spent most of the night studying a map of the area. In the morning Secretary of War Thomas J. Rusk joined Houston's forces. On this day Houston addressed the troops.

"It's come, men. This is the moment you've been waiting for. This is where we attack Santa Anna's forces," Houston told the eager troops.

At last they were going to get their chance to even things up. And the cries went out, "Remember the Alamo!" "Remember Goliad!"

Houston's scout, Deaf Smith, swam across the bayou. When he returned at dusk, he had great news for his general.

"General Houston, Sir, General Santa Anna has only about eight hundred men with him. The rest of his forces under General Cos are following slowly behind him. We can take them, Sir, I'm sure of it!" Deaf Smith told Houston.

Santa Anna was on his way to Morgan's Point. He had missed Burnet and his government. They were on Galveston Island before Santa Anna could reach them.

Now Houston got out his maps again. This time he was sure. He had the Mexicans in a corner. They could not get out of this without a fight. At last he had them where he wanted them.

He left his sick and disabled men in camp. The rest of the men took up a brutal march. They crossed the Buffalo Bayou, then Vince's Bayou by a bridge, and marched on in the dark.

"From here on, there must be no talking. Try to muffle the sound of your arms," commanded Houston. He did not want Santa Anna to know about their march. At two o'clock the men were allowed to rest for awhile. But it was not for long. Scouts reported that Santa Anna was moving his men in the direction of Lynch's Ferry, about eight miles northeast of Morgan's Point. Houston took up the race for the ferry. If Houston got there first, Santa Anna would have to fight or lead his forces into the marshes toward the west.

Houston won the race. By late morning his army took its position in a grove of oak trees. Before him were two miles of prairie covered with green grass and clumps of timber. At last there was time for breakfast for Houston's troops. However, they did not get to finish eating.

The Mexicans had placed a single cannon on a slope at the edge of the prairie. Colonel Sherman asked permission to capture the cannon. Houston refused, but gave Sherman permission to check on the Mexican position. Just as Sherman's party rode out of sight, Houston heard shots.

"What's that firing about?" shouted Houston.

"Sherman's charged the Mexican line," Deaf Smith answered.

Santa Anna's troops dashed up and drove Sherman and his men back. One man was killed and two others were wounded. During the flare-up Mirabeau B. Lamar

rode into the fight and rescued one of the injured men.
"Lamar has him, Sir," said one of the men to Houston.
"He does, indeed," Houston answered. "That man is a good soldier. Promote him to the rank of colonel at once!" Briefly he remembered his own promotion by Andrew Jackson. It seemed a very long time since Horseshoe Bend.

Things settled down after the brief fight. The Mexicans made their camp a short distance away. Houston's men, dog-tired, cooked their meal and then settled down to rest. Just before dawn, Houston's men stood waiting for Houston to awaken. He slept until sunrise.

"Isn't he ever going to get up?" asked one of the officers.

"We were all tired, but he's overdoing it," answered another. "I don't believe he knows what he's doing. It's high time to attack, if we're ever going to do it."

Finally Houston aroused himself and ate his breakfast. About this time Deaf Smith rode into camp.

"General, the army under General Cos is approaching. He has several hundred men with him," Smith informed the General.

"They probably have us outnumbered," Houston said. "But fortune's with us this day."

Houston called Smith aside so that the men would not hear his instructions. His plan would certainly call for objections from his own men.

"Smith, you take D. W. Reeves with you. I want you to go back to Vince's Bridge and destroy it," Houston ordered.

"But, Sir, that's our only line of retreat," objected Deaf Smith.

"Well, it's certain no one, least of all the Mexicans, can use it then," answered Houston.

Smith's face wrinkled into a grin of delight.

"This'll make a real good fight, Sir," said Smith.

"Well, you'll have to hurry, or you'll miss the fun," Houston said, checking the blade of his sword.

After Smith and Reeves had left the camp, Houston chose a young soldier who could beat time on a drum.

"Is there anyone who can play a fife?" asked Houston.

At once the men pushed a young man forward.

"Can you play a tune?" asked Houston.

"Sir, I'm not very good. The only tune I know is "Will You Come to the Bower," answered the young man. He had learned a popular love song of the day.

The general smiled grimly and said, "That tune will do just fine. Just play loud so that we can all hear it."

But still the general delayed the attack. The men began to fear he did not intend to make an attack. The longer he waited, the more certain they were.

However, they did not reckon with the general's Indian capacity to lie in wait. He wanted just the right time. He called his officers together and let them list their objections. Finally, he dismissed them. He had bought enough time. At half past three Houston gave the order to "arm and line." The fight was on.

There was no sign of life from the Mexican camp. It was their siesta time. Even Santa Anna was in his tent. Some of the soldiers were gathering wood for their campfires. Many were asleep in the shade of the trees. The only soldiers on horses were those leading the mounts to water.

The struggle in the front line was brief. The Mexicans never had a chance to form for battle. The Texans were shouting "Remember the Alamo! Remember Goliad!" as they swarmed over the Mexican defense.

The enemy forces fled out over the prairie in wild retreat. The Texas cavalry were right behind them. Many of the Mexicans died in the muddy, foul water of the bayou. Everything was in confusion. Santa Anna was so startled by the action that he was unable to give orders. Dressed in red slippers and a blue dressing gown, he mounted a horse and dashed off toward Vince's Bridge.

Some Texas cavalrymen pursued him, but he escaped by turning his horse loose and trying to slip away on foot.

The next day he was spotted. He told the men who found him that he was a Mexican cavalryman.

His ruse was of no use. His own men recognized him. A large group of Mexican prisoners, sitting on the ground as he passed, jumped to their feet. They shouted, "El Presidente! El Presidente!"

So they had him. As he was led to Houston, who had suffered a leg injury, the Texas forces gathered around. Their angry faces showed their feelings about the man.

"Hang him right now," they shouted. "Kill the butcher of the Alamo!"

"He does not deserve to live this long," shouted one man.

Houston lay propped under an oak tree. He tried to calm the threats of the men.

"He'll receive his just dues," Houston told the soldiers. "He is a prisoner now. We'll wait for the courts to decide his fate."

Houston knew that Santa Anna was worth more to Texas as a prisoner than he would be dead. His life could serve as a bargaining tool to keep down other attacks from Mexico.

Santa Anna's force was wiped out. Only about forty Mexicans succeeded in escaping. As for the Texans, two men were killed and twenty-three were wounded. The war was over. Texas was free at last!

CHAPTER SIX

"General Houston, Sir, there's a lady out here to see you. She's angry as an old wet hen, Sir," said the orderly. He knew the general did not feel like seeing a lady with problems, but there seemed no other way to be rid of her.

"That's all I need, Boy. Well, let's see if we can get rid of her," the general answered. "Show her in."

"General Houston, I want them smelly Mexicans out of my pasture," the lady shouted at him as she entered the tent. "I can't stand to live there with all them bodies around."

"Ma'm, we're doing the best we can," answered Houston, trying not to smile at her frantic air. Of course, she wanted her farm cleaned up. "Just give us a little time. We'll try to help you, but in the meantime, just try to bear with us."

"Thank you, Sir," said the orderly as he escorted the woman from the tent.

"I don't know, Smith," Houston turned to his friend, Deaf Smith, "just what we can do about all the problems of these people. However, there's a worse problem facing us. I just got a message this morning that Burnet's on his way here from Galveston."

"Sir, he's transferred his offices to Velasco," answered Smith. "He's fit to be tied because Santa Anna's still alive. I heard as much from the messenger himself."

Many Texans felt that Houston had been too generous in his treatment of the Mexican leader. However, the general was sure that alive, Santa Anna was worth much more than his corpse would be. He could use the man to bargain with the rest of the Mexican nation. Actually, President Burnet could see that Houston was too popular with the people. That might cause him problems in the next election. He did not want that to happen.

President Burnet growled at the general when he was escorted into Houston's presence.

"I don't know why you haven't executed the butcher!" Burnet shouted at Houston when they met.

"Sir, I have plans for the man. I want to assure you that Texas will remain free from Mexican armies such as this," Houston assured the president.

"Well, perhaps you'll change you mind after you hear from the rest of Texas," answered Burnet shortly. "I want to take the government back to Galveston. I will take Santa Anna along with us. We'll sail on the *Yellowstone* tomorrow."

"Mr. President, Sir, I'd like to accompany you if I may. I need to have a doctor look at my leg wound," asked Houston.

Burnet turned toward the door without an answer.

On May 6, 1836, Houston was told that he would not be allowed to sail on the *Yellowstone* with the rest of the government. When Houston's doctor heard the message, he went at once to the captain of the *Yellowstone.*

"Captain, this man must have passage! I can't give him the care he needs. The hero of San Jacinto is likely to die right here on the battlefield if we don't get him to New Orleans as soon as possible," the doctor told the captain.

"It's my ship, and I will refuse to sail if he's not on board. Of that you may be assured," the captain answered.

Late in the afternoon of May 7, the two Rusk brothers, Thomas and David, carried Houston's cot aboard the ship. Burnet's officials made no objections. Houston's men might take over the ship if they refused!

At Galveston another setback was in store for Houston. He was refused passage on a Texas naval vessel to

New Orleans. Finally on May 11 he obtained passage on a leaky merchant ship, the *Flora*. Houston's arrival in New Orleans was certainly a change from Galveston. People gathered at the docks to greet the hero of San Jacinto. Houston himself was almost unconscious from pain. Nevertheless, he managed to hobble ashore with help.

On the dock to meet him was a friend, William Christy.

"Sam, my friend, it's good to see you, in spite of the condition you're in," said Christy. He helped Houston to the carriage that he had waiting.

Doubled over with pain, Houston tried to mumble his thanks. The effort was almost too much for him. He was taken at once to the doctors that Christy had waiting. After the surgery Houston was taken to Christy's home for his recovery. Although he was very weak after the doctors repaired his leg, Houston received many callers. They came to wish him well and to compliment him on his success at San Jacinto.

"The eyes of the entire nation are upon you," Christy told his visitor. "Everyone is excited about your new nation."

"I know, Sir, and that's just the reason I have to be on my way. My new nation needs guidance. It's in real trouble," answered Houston.

"But, Sam, your leg is not healed," said Christy. "It's far from well. Traveling will be hard on you."

On his way to Nacogdoches, Houston passed through Natchitoches, Louisiana, where he met Dr. Robert Irion. Irion traveled with Houston to Nacogdoches. There Houston introduced Irion to the beautiful Anna Raguet. It was almost love at first sight. They fell deeply in love. Within a few years they were married.

After President Burnet issued a call for a general election, Houston's name was offered for president. A group of citizens from San Augustine were sure he could win. Houston was elected without lifting a finger. The honor was thrust upon the hero of San Jacinto.

As president, Houston's first problem was what to

do with Santa Anna. A series of letters were written between Houston and Andrew Jackson. Through Jackson's efforts, Santa Anna was sent to Washington. From there Jackson had Santa Anna put aboard a naval vessel bound for Veracruz, Mexico. That problem was solved.

However, Houston's problems with Mexico were not over. Many of the San Jacinto veterans were unemployed. They were roaming about Texas. General Felix Huston decided to get them to join him in a filibuster against Mexico. That meant more trouble!

Then there was the problem of annexation to the United States. Houston wanted it, but the problem of slavery kept the question unsettled for another decade. Texas had slaves and the North feared upsetting the balance of power. In the meantime Houston decided to move the capital city from Columbia to Houston City, named for himself.

On December 13, 1838, Mirabeau B. Lamar became the second president of the Republic of Texas. Shortly after the first of the year, Houston planned a trip to the United States. In New Orleans he received a royal reception. This time he was well enough to enjoy all the honors paid him.

From New Orleans Houston sailed to Mobile, Alabama. There he met a gentleman named William Bledsoe. Houston hoped to interest Bledsoe in investing in a project to build Sabine City. Bledsoe liked Houston. He invited him to visit his home in Spring Hill.

"Sir, I hope that you will give us the pleasure of your company at a little garden party," said Bledsoe. His wife was entertaining the ladies of the local Baptist Church. "I would like you to meet my mother-in-law, Nancy Lea. Perhaps she will be interested in the Sabine City project."

"Thank you very much. I shall enjoy the treat of a visit with the ladies," Houston answered. Houston did not even guess the treat that was in store for him.

It was a May afternoon when Bledsoe brought General Houston to his stately home. There Houston met Antoinette, Bledsoe's eighteen-year-old wife. Then Bledsoe moved toward Antoinette's sister, Margaret Lea, who was serving strawberries and cream to the guests.

" General Houston, I want you to meet our sister, Margaret Lea," Bledsoe said. The dark-haired, violet-eyed Margaret curtsied to the general. He took her hand, helping her up from the deep bow. The pale-featured young girl smiled at him and his heart was lost. Shortly afterwards he asked her to show him the gardens at Spring Hill. Antoinette was amused when she saw very little of them that afternoon.

They had much to talk about. Margaret had read about General Houston. She had many questions to ask him. Houston was charmed by her knowledge and interest.

However, Nancy Lea was not charmed by her daughter's interest in this man. She too had heard a great deal about Sam Houston.

"I tell you, Antoinette, she's spending too much time with that man," complained Nancy Lea. "It's not good. He's entirely too old for her."

"But, Mama, Margaret knows about him. She will not be indiscreet," answered Antoinette.

"Well, I don't know. I just don't like it," Nancy Lea said. "I am interested in that project of his at Sabine City. Otherwise I'd send him packing right now."

Nancy Lea was interested in Sabine City and Texas. So much so that she sent her son-in-law, William, to Texas to check on the project. Bledsoe was told to invest a large amount of her money if he liked the project. Houston remained in Mobile. He was completely wrapped up in the charming Margaret.

Nancy Lea realized that her daughter was considering Houston's proposal. Early in June she decided to take her daughter home to Marion, Alabama. When Houston heard of the plan to go home, he suggested to Margaret that they marry at once.

"Mr. Houston, I can't do my family that way," answered Margaret. "I have to prepare them for what we want to do."

"But, Margaret, can't you do that here in Mobile?" asked the eager Sam Houston.

"No, my love, you must come to Marion to meet my relatives and friends there. It's only proper that you do," Margaret said firmly.

Margaret got her way. Houston would do anything she asked. She and her mother went to Marion to make plans for Houston's later visit. Houston himself went on to Nashville to visit with his old friend, Andrew Jackson. The two old friends had much to talk about, such as Horseshoe Bend, the Battle of New Orleans, San Jacinto.

"Sam, my son, I've waited long for your story about the retreat before San Jacinto," Andrew Jackson told his friend. "Just why did it take so long?"

"Sir, you know as well as I that a smaller force has to have some advantage," answered Houston thoughtfully. "I knew that we had to have them at the right spot and the right time. You know that the Mexicans are fond of their siesta?"

"That I've heard often," answered Jackson.

"Well, Sir, I just had to wait until exactly the right time," Houston said. "There near the bayou, we had them cornered. I destroyed the bridge that might lead to their escape. Then we just waited until they were resting before attacking."

"Indeed, you were smart, my friend, to pick such a time for the fight. Your choosing the prudent course about executing Santa Anna was another mark in your favor," Andrew Jackson said.

The two old friends talked on into the night about many matters, especially the annexation of Texas.

"I feel certain that eventually the matter of annexation will be solved. We just have this troublesome matter of slavery to solve. It will be soon, I hope," Jackson told him. "For one thing, the United States can't afford to have another Canada on its border."

"Sir, I have another matter to talk about," Houston said eagerly. "I want your approval very much. I have been much taken by a young lady in Alabama. I intend to marry her as soon as I can secure her family's approval."

On July 17, 1839, Houston received a letter from Margaret. Its contents disappointed him. "I regret deeply that I will not be able to see you in Mobile. However, my sister and brother-in-law will be happy to see you. Mother and William are going to Texas, but my mother does not want me to go with them. You must visit me here in Marion before she will agree to my going."

Within the month Houston was headed toward the town of Marion. Nothing could have kept him from visiting Margaret on his way back to Texas.

"Mr. Houston, I am so glad to see you again. I did so hope that you would come to Marion," said a radiant Margaret.

"My dear Margaret, I couldn't go back to Texas without seeing you again," Houston answered. He knew that this lively girl would change his life. She made it clear that she planned to do so. Margaret was just the girl who could!

Houston was well received in Marion. However, Margaret's mother and her brother Henry were not completely charmed. He proposed again to Margaret, but her family insisted that they wait. The family hoped Margaret would change her mind. With that, Sam Houston had to be satisfied. One thing was certain, he would have to make another trip to Mobile before he could win the charming Margaret.

From Mobile Houston went back to Nacogdoches. There he was enraged at the tales his friends told him.

"General Houston, you know how Lamar hates the Indians?" said Henry Raguet. "He waited until you were gone before he started his plan."

"Right after you left, he started a series of small wars against the Indians," added Adolphus Sterne. "He was determined to drive them out of the country."

"I knew he hated them, but I didn't think he would go this far," Houston answered, grinding his heel into the dirt.

"What he did was stir them up," added Raguet. "He allowed surveyors for the land traders to go into Cherokee lands."

"But even that did not stir them up enough," put in Sterne. "Finally, they caught some of the Bowl's men helping a Mexican bandit named Manuel Flores. They accused Chief Bowl of helping Santa Anna against Texas."

"Poor old Bowl. He was eighty-three years old. He was too old to lead his men into war," Houston sighed as he spoke of his old friend.

"But they forced him into war. He had to lead his people. His order to attack came on July 15, 1839," Sterne told Houston. "Bowl led the charge himself. He rode up and down encouraging his warriors. When the battle finally ended, Captain Robert Smith shot the old fellow in the back as he hobbled from the field."

"And then the troops chased the other Indians, all of them, men, women, and children to the Arkansas line," added Raguet.

After expressing his outrage over Bowl's death, Houston mounted his horse and rode toward Austin. He had been elected to the House of Representatives. Lamar had moved the capital city back to Austin.

"This move is a most unfortunate thing," Houston told a friend. "It may be beautiful here, but we're subject to Mexican as well as Indian raids."

"Sir, you know the land promoters hope to sell more lots in Austin," answered the friend.

"All I can say is that the capital should not have been moved," Houston remarked. "The term of years is not up yet. Anyway, the people should vote on where the capital is located."

Lamar was in trouble. He insisted on promoting the Mexican war. He had caused the Indians to continue their savage raids. He had issued large sums of paper money known as "red backs." The red backs tumbled in value to sixteen cents on the dollar within the year. Finally, he dreamed of a great conquest that would bring him glory. He would send an expedition to Santa Fe to set up trade there. He dreamed about this for months before he set it into action.

The year 1840 brought Houston the wife he wanted. After several different dates were set, he finally went to Marion, Alabama, where he and Margaret were married on May 9, 1840.

After the wedding breakfast, the Houstons retired to the Lafayette Hotel in Marion. There they remained for a week while Margaret's belongings were packed and crated. They were entertained at several parties, such as a barbecue in a grove near the Baptist graveyard. When they finally left Marion, Eliza, Margaret's black servant, went with them. Three other slaves would go to Texas with Martin Lea, Margaret's brother.

While they were on their way to Texas, Margaret talked with Sam about his drinking.

"Mr. Houston, I do sincerely hope you will give up this terrible habit," the young bride told her husband. She had made up her mind that he must not drink again. Margaret knew that the habit had caused him much trouble already.

"Margaret, my dear, you know that I would do anything for you," Sam told his bride. "I can't promise that I will never drink again, but I can promise that I will not drink to excess. I will never be drunk again!"

Margaret accepted his promise happily. She would work to see that he did not want to drink again. Sam was deliriously fond of this young woman who planned to rule his life.

CHAPTER SEVEN

The honeymoon for the Houstons did not last long. Houston had to return to the Redlands to campaign for his House seat.

"But, Mr. Houston, we've had such a short time together," his bride complained. "It seems a shame that you have to leave so soon."

"Margaret, my dearest, I have to support my family now," Houston answered, smiling at his beloved wife. "I shall have to go to Austin for the session of Congress after I win."

He and Margaret were sitting on the porch of her mother's home in Galveston. They were watching the colorful sunset over the Gulf of Mexico. Usually, Houston did not talk about business affairs with Margaret. However, he felt the need to tell her about one of his problems.

"I know you don't care for politics, Margaret, but there is a big problem facing our nation," Houston said. "I feel that you should know about it."

He told her about President Lamar's plan to send the group of traders to New Mexico. Lamar intended to take up trade with the area surrounding Santa Fe. Congress had already turned the plan down once. But Lamar was now proposing that it would be a peace mission. Soldiers would go with the members only to protect them. A government would be set up in the territory.

"But, Mr. Houston, why on earth would Texas even consider an expedition like that," Margaret asked. "We have more than enough land already."

"Well, you see, they make excellent wine at El Paso

del Norte. The grape growers there are raising a choice kind of grape," Houston paused, watching Margaret's face. "They send wine and brandy through New Mexico and up the Santa Fe Trail. The duties and charges bring in much money for Mexico. Lamar hopes to take over that trade. The money would bail out our failing Texas economy."

"I know enough, my husband, to understand the danger that it might bring to Texas," answered a doubtful Margaret. "We've already had enough of that murderer, Santa Anna. We don't want him here again."

With that Houston had made up his mind. He could hardly wait for the next session of Congress. He would oppose the Lamar plan. His first speech there blasted the plan.

"Gentlemen, you would be out of your minds if you take this idea seriously," Houston roared. "It is a thousand miles to Santa Fe. It is a land filled with wilderness, mountains, and murderous Indians. Why send these men to their certain deaths?"

Again Congress refused to support Lamar's plan. But Lamar had a way around the Congress. He had printed $500,000 in currency. With this paper money, he intended to pay for the trip to Santa Fe. In June the group was on its way, headed by Colonel Hugh McLeod. There were 270 soldiers, a few merchants, and a reporter from the New Orleans *Picayune*.

Before the end of Houston's term in the legislature, he had made up his mind to run again for president. There was no Texan that summer of 1841 who could have defeated Sam Houston. The election was a runaway for Houston. He defeated David Burnet by a margin of better than two to one. The parties in his honor were many. At Washington-on-the-Brazos thirteen hogs and two large steers were barbecued. Many of his friends were surprised to find that Houston was not drinking any more. But he was keeping his promise to Margaret. He loved her dearly. Almost never again was alcohol to devil him.

Margaret was not in Austin to see her husband sworn in. She remained in Houston City. Houston appeared at the ceremony in a hunting shirt, an old pair of pants, and an old, wide-brimmed fur hat. He spoke of industry and economy as the means to save Texas. Among the measures of economy he announced that he would not live in a rich mansion which Lamar had built. He made his home at the Eberly House instead.

Houston's plans for economy were greeted with wild enthusiasm. Texans knew that their state was in great trouble. Salaries were reduced. Taxes were cut in half. Even Houston's own salary was cut in half.

Moreover, Houston was worried about the safety of the capital. Comanche raids just outside of Austin had destroyed settlers' homes and property, as well as their lives. Too, nothing would please Santa Anna more than to capture the top officers of the Texan government. He would love parading them through the streets of Mexico City, especially Sam Houston, his bitter enemy.

Suddenly, however, the whole country was shaken by the news from the Santa Fe Expedition. The men suffered miserably from the lack of food, illness, and betrayal by their Mexican guide. Then on October 9, 1841, they were captured by Governor Armijo's army. They were marched into the place before San Miguel Church. There, starving and ill, their clothes were taken away from them. They were given one blanket each to cover themselves. Most were without shoes. All of the men expected to be killed.

However, they were told that they must march on foot to Mexico City, two thousand miles away. If one of the men became sick or tired on the road, he would be shot and his ears cut off. The ears were kept to provide a count of the prisoners lost. News of the expedition poured into Texas and the United States. People were filled with anger at the horror of the march.

Houston began at once to start efforts to help the prisoners. He talked with the British agent at Galveston. He hoped to persuade the British minister in Mexico City to help the prisoners. However, he refused to declare war on Mexico. Texas was not prepared to carry out a war. It was one thing to fight in Texas; quite another to fight in Mexico! But Congress did not agree. It turned its rage on the president. They were ready to impeach Houston.

Santa Anna did not wait long to punish Texas for the Santa Fe Expedition. On March 6, 1842, General Rafael Vasquez brought his fourteen hundred troops across the Rio Grande. They took San Antonio and captured one hundred prisoners whom they took back to Mexico City.

Houston called General Alexander Somervell into his office.

"General, I want you to take charge of the troops that I am sending to the Rio Grande," Houston said. "But you must be firm with the men. They must not cross the Rio Grande. We are not prepared to fight a war. We do not have the rifles, lead, and powder at the present time."

"Sir, you know the mood of the troops," General Somervell answered. "It will be hard to keep them back. They are very bitter about Santa Fe."

"Keep them back regardless, Sir," answered Houston. "Send two companies of fifty-six men each to scout the border. Have them report any movement of the Mexican armies."

Despite Houston's efforts, the cry for war continued. He told the public that the country did not have the funds to carry out a war. But nothing helped to quiet the outcry. Finally, Houston issued orders for a militia to carry out a defensive war.

Among other things Houston ordered that the capital be moved from Austin back to Houston City. He was especially afraid that the archives, all of the documents and papers that had been kept since the beginning of the government, would be destroyed by the enemy. This was the beginning of "The Archives War."

"They just want to move the capital," said one Austin citizen. "If they take those papers, they'll never bring them back."

"Well, we had best see that they don't take them," said another. "I say that we ought to hide them away somewhere safe!"

With that purpose in mind, the citizens of Austin did bury the papers in trunks. They intended to keep the archives in Austin, in spite of what the president might do.

Meanwhile the struggle with Mexico continued. The administration decided that the government would be safer at Washington-on-the-Brazos. So plans were made to move there. Just as they were ready to leave Houston City, a messenger rode up to the president's house. He brought the news that Santa Anna had made his second bid for revenge. Colonel Adrian Woll had raided San Antonio with fourteen hundred men. When Woll withdrew, he took away all the property he could carry and fifty prisoners.

Houston sent about twelve hundred men to relieve the Alamo city. The first two hundred soldiers to arrive were met at the outskirts of the town by a much larger Mexican army. The Texans, however, drove them off with a terrific fight. By the time they entered the town, the Mexicans were gone.

"It's time he did something, I say," spoke one of Houston's critics. "They just can't keep on taking prisoners without his doing something about it!"

But the country waited in vain for the ringing appeal from their president. He did order two regiments of militia and any United States volunteers still in the country to assemble at San Antonio. General Somervell was ordered to prepare for defense. Galveston got ready for possible defense at sea. Houston was eager to punish Colonel Woll, but he wanted to keep the country out of war.

In the meantime the government prepared for its

move to Washington-on-the-Brazos. Six wagons, each drawn by three yoke of oxen, carried the belongings from Houston City. Mrs. Houston rode on one of the wagons along with her piano and her harp. They reached Washington on October 3rd. The trip was long and hard, especially on Margaret.

The town of Washington was not prepared for the sudden arrival of so many people. Houses were rapidly being built. But there was not a suitable house for the president. He and Mrs. Houston were invited to stay at the home of friends, the Lockharts. Mrs. Lockhart gave them her best room which she had furnished with her prized possessions. She even put her pride and joy, a four-poster bed, in the room. There was a side door, cut into the wall so that the Houstons could have a private entrance.

Now that he was settled once again, Houston made another attempt to get the archives moved. On October 8th, he issued an order to have the papers moved. The order was ignored by the citizens of Austin.

Finally Houston sent Captain Thomas Smith and a group of men to Austin to remove the papers secretly. At midnight, Mrs. Angelina Eberly, the boarding house mistress, saw wagons being loaded in an alley behind the land office. She ran out to Congress Avenue. A cannon had been kept there since the days of the Indian wars. She turned the muzzle of the cannon toward the land office and fired a shot. The shot hit the building and woke up the whole town.

Captain Smith and his wagoners drove off with the papers they had loaded. They were stopped a little distance out of town. The papers were returned to Austin. The wagoners were treated to a special supper at Mrs. Eberly's house, and the Archives War was over. Houston was forced to give up or risk the destruction of the papers entirely. The handful of Austin citizens who held the archives against so many odds were probably responsible for making Austin the permanent capital of Texas.

CHAPTER EIGHT

Trouble with Mexico continued. Finally, on December 3, General Somervell sent his troops across the Rio Grande. They moved into Laredo, capturing the town without many losses. Somervell then brought his little force back to Texas soil.

William S. Fisher, who had been Lamar's secretary of war complained. "General, we haven't hurt them enough. We'd better do a good job of it, or they'll be right back again," said Fisher.

"Fisher, you know we do not have enough men. We will do well to hold them below the Rio Grande," answered Somervell.

"Well, I don't know about that," replied Fisher.

At once Fisher began gathering as many of the troops as he could. He sold them on the idea of gaining gold and glory in Mexico.

"We can do it easily, men," he told them.

Three hundred men set off with Fisher on December 19th. They reached the town of Mier by Christmas Eve. General Pedro Ampudia and his Mexican forces met and thrashed the Texans severely.

The Texans were then marched to Matamoros. There they were paraded through the streets. The same thing happened in other river towns. Then the prisoners were tied together with lariats. In this manner they were marched to Mexico City by way of Monterrey and Saltillo. Santa Anna had told General Canales and Ampudia to execute one in every ten of the men.

In order to choose those to be executed, black beans

were placed in a jar with white beans. The prisoners were made to draw the beans from the jar. Those having black beans were to be executed. The black beans were placed on top of the white beans. Then the officers were made to draw first. General Canales hoped to get rid of the officers. But the officers reached deep into the beans and drew out white beans.

The men to be shot were marched into a courtyard. There they were fired upon. Some were hit as many as fifteen times. The rest of the prisoners were marched to Mexico City and put into prisons.

Houston was blamed for the fiasco. After all, he had sent General Somervell to the Rio Grande. Disorder reigned in Texas. Some of the western Texans rose in fury against Houston's authority.

One day while Margaret Houston was away in Grand Cane, the president happened to pass Hatfield's saloon. The saloon keeper hailed him and invited him to come in. Houston accepted the invitation freely. After all, everyone knew that the president no longer drank.

"Sir, I just want to show you this fine Madeira wine. I just received it in my last shipment from New Orleans," said the saloon owner. "It's by far the best we've seen in months."

"Indeed, it does have a fine color," answered Houston.

"Well, sir, I would like to present you with a gallon," the proud owner said. He held out a jug of wine to Houston.

"No, sir, I cannot accept it," Houston answered, thinking what a fine gift it was. "But I will take it for my landlord's wife. I'm sure Mrs. Lockhart will enjoy it."

Houston was glad to find something unusual to repay Mrs. Lockhart for her kindness. Unfortunately, when Houston reached the Lockhart house, Mrs. Lockhart was not at home. He had made up his mind to give a little speech in presenting the wine. So he set the jug by the door of his room leading into the Lockharts' part of the house.

Whatever happened next is not clear. Probably he looked at the jug for a long time. Sometime in the night he decided to sample the wine. One sample led to another. About two o'clock he decided that one of the bedposts was keeping him from breathing freely. He called his servant Joshua to bring an ax. Together they chopped off a post at the foot of the bed, Mrs. Lockhart's treasured bed!

Judge Lockhart, awakened by the noise, rushed into Houston's room. "General Houston, are you all right?" he asked.

"I am indeed," answered the befuddled Houston.

"Then, Sir, I'd suggest that you get back into bed. Joshua go on back to your bed, too," said the startled Mr. Lockhart.

Houston, satisfied that he had improved his sleeping quarters, climbed back into the bed. He was soon snoring away.

This seems to have been Houston's last binge. However, he did not get off lightly. The story raced through the capital. Once again they were calling Houston "Big Drunk." He worried about what Margaret would think. But Margaret knew that she would never leave him alone again. She knew he needed her with him at all times.

Early in 1843 Santa Anna released a prisoner, James W. Robinson. Robinson returned to Texas with the Mexican's terms for freeing the prisoners in Perote prison. He went directly to Washington-on-the-Brazos to talk with Houston.

The United States government was alarmed when on June 15, 1843, Houston announced that an armistice with Mexico had been secured. It would be in force while they worked for a lasting peace.

"I tell you, Sir, we could have won the land between here and the Pacific if old Sam had just gone ahead and fought," said one critic. "All we had to do was whip them Mexicans again!"

"And we could to it, too," answered his friend.

"Well, one thing is certain. Seems like he wants to do away with slavery here in Texas," said the first man.

"I hear the congressmen from West Texas have called a convention," announced a latecomer to the talk.

"That ought to let old Sam know how the country feels," added the first man.

But Sam himself was wrapped up in the birth of his first son on May 25, 1843. Margaret insisted that the boy be called Sam, Jr. Nancy Lea insisted upon bringing the family food and provisions from Houston City.

"Nancy, I don't feel it's right for you to do this," said an embarrassed Sam Houston. "You must not supply us with food."

"Now, Mr. Houston, you be embarrassed if you want to," answered Nancy Lea. "But my grandson is not old enough to do without the things he needs. For his good and for your own, you had better just take the food. You can pay me back later."

By early fall Sam Houston announced an agreement with Santa Anna. They would exchange prisoners. This announcement brought about a change in the United States. They decided that they should annex Texas. The country might just find out it could exist without U.S. aid. Santa Anna then announced that if the U.S. annexed Texas, he would begin war in earnest.

However, Houston refused to make a public statement in favor of annexation. He felt that the United States had not adopted a course he could accept. He said the U.S. must annex Texas. Texas could not annex herself to the United States. Finally on February 16, 1844, Houston wrote to Jackson that he was ready to accept annexation. But as he said, "The bride at the altar should not be jilted by the groom." Finally by April 12th President Tyler finally submitted his annexation treaty to the Senate. The treaty now became a political football for the opposing parties.

In the meantime William Bledsoe's property was in danger of being lost. Because of his financial difficulties, the title to the land was transferred to Nancy Lea. At first it was thought that Houston might buy it. However, he was trying to buy a piece of land near Huntsville. That was the place he had chosen for his retirement. While the slavery question was debated in Washington, the Houstons moved into a house they called Raven Hill. Here, fifteen miles from Huntsville, Margaret thought they would live out their lives in peace.

On February 20, 1845, four days before Polk's inauguration, the United States Congress consented to the annexation. Shortly after this event Houston learned that his friend, Andrew Jackson, was dying. Houston decided to take his family to see the great man.

They left for the Hermitage in early April. The Houstons disembarked at New Orleans during the last week in May. They visited for a short while with William Christy. Houston spoke to the local businessmen while they were there. He said that he had been accused of favoring England and France.

"I was only flirting with them," he told the man. "My heart has always been with the Union."

When they left for Nashville, they did not know that they were in a race with death. Andrew Jackson had become much worse. On June 8, 1845, Andrew Jackson died. The Houstons arrived a few hours after his death. Sam Houston took his young son into Jackson's bedroom.

"My son, I want you always to remember that you looked on the face of a great man," Houston told his son, holding him close.

After Jackson's funeral, the Houstons visited in Nashville for almost two months. They were entertained by old friends and even by those who had once opposed Houston. Now, Houston was a hero in the United States. On June 28th the Texas Congress approved the annexation on American terms.

CHAPTER NINE

From Nashville the Houstons had gone to Marion, Alabama, to visit Margaret's family. It was while they were there that Houston had some unsettling news. Santa Anna had broken off relations with the United States.

"Margaret, I hate to leave you and young Sam here," Houston told his wife, "but I am needed in Texas."

What he did not tell her at the time was that his name had been submitted for senator from the new state. He had to go home to campaign. Houston knew how unhappy Margaret would be. She enjoyed having him at home with her. She truly disliked public life.

Houston's election did not come as a surprise to anyone. The family was at Raven Hill when the news came on February 25, 1846.

"My dear, we will have to go to Washington," Houston said. "We have about three weeks to get ready to leave. I'm sure it will be a great adventure for you."

"But, Mr. Houston, I do not want to go," answered the unhappy Margaret. Before the time came to leave, Margaret found an excuse. She was to have their second child. The trip would be too hard on her.

"I promise, Mr. Houston, that I will follow you after the baby is born," said Margaret.

However, she never made the trip during all the years he served in Washington. Houston was sworn in as senator on March 30, 1846. He had come to Washington aboard a jolting train, after twenty-six hundred miles from Houston.

Houston looked up at the familiar sign as he entered

the door of Brown's Hotel. Pocahontas' face was still on the sign although it was no longer called the "Indian Queen Hotel." He thought of earlier days when he had stayed there.

"Mr. Houston, it's good to see you back," said Jesse Brown, the bartender turned owner. "Here, have a drink for old times' sake."

"Jesse, it's good to see you," answered Houston, "but I won't have the drink. I don't touch the stuff any more."

"That's certainly a change from the past, Mr. Houston," said Jesse.

The problems facing the United States during Houston's thirteen years in the Senate were many. Among the problems were the Oregon boundary questions and the Mexican War over Texas' boundary. But the most pressing problem was that of slavery. The fight was raging in Congress.

Margaret Houston was still at Raven Hill in May. She was afraid of the effect the Mexican War would have upon her family. Houston could hardly wait until Congress adjourned on August 10th. He wanted very much to go to Texas to be with Margaret and young Sam. He was at home at Raven Hill when their second child, Nancy Elizabeth, was born.

"Mr. Houston, I know that you have to return to Washington," Margaret told Sam. "However, I want you to think about selling this house. It's too far from town. I don't like living out here alone with the servants and the children."

"Margaret, I have been thinking about it. I am making arrangements to buy a house much nearer Huntsville," Houston told her. "It will be easier for you there. You can attend church on Sundays. You'll like that, won't you?"

"Dearest, I knew you would understand," Margaret said.

"Well, I know you'll like it. Really, it's a bang-up good place," Houston added. It did indeed become their favorite home.

Houston spent that Christmas at home. He wanted Margaret to go back to Washington with him, but again she refused. At last she had a house that she liked much better than Raven Hill.

On February 2, 1848, the Mexican delegates signed a treaty of peace at Guadalupe Hidalgo in Mexico. The trouble with Mexico was finally ended for Texas.

During all of Houston's stay in the U.S. Senate, slavery was the main problem facing the nation. Houston's heart was with the Union. Just as Andrew Jackson before him, he said. "The Union, it must be preserved!" He fought to save the Union. When Houston was finally defeated in his bid for reelection to the Senate, he returned home. His service in Washington was at an end.

However, things at home were not the same. Houston had made great debts during his campaign. They were forced to sell the Huntsville house and return to Independence. They still had a house and property there.

In October while Margaret was making plans for their move to Independence, Houston spent some time with his friend, Ashbel Smith. They were sitting in the warm October sunshine outside the house in Huntsville.

"General, you're right about the sheep. You can double your money in a couple of years," said Smith. They were both whittling on slabs of pine. For Houston this was a way to relax while thinking through a problem.

"I think I can do it easily," answered Houston cutting a long sliver of pine from the slab. "I have never liked farming very much. But I think I can manage a small sheep ranch at Cedar Point. You know, I have over four thousand acres of land there."

"What are you going to do about running for governor?" asked Smith. "You know, we need your help. This is going to be a change for Texas. Being governor won't be like it was as president."

"It's going to be hard for everyone. This slavery thing is really out of hand. I want Texas to stay in the

Union," answered Houston. "It seems though that a bunch of hotheads will insist on secession."

"I hope you think long and hard about it," Smith urged.

"Well, you know there's one who won't like my running," Houston added. "Margaret thinks I spend too much time away from my family. I don't want to hurt her any more. But you're right. Texas will need a strong hand to guide her through these bad times.

Houston did run for governor. His campaign consisted of one published letter and one public speech. He tried to please Margaret in every way. In fact, he spent most of the summer with the family at Cedar Point. The last half of 1859 was a great joy to Margaret. She had her family together without politics separating them. But then Houston did win the election.

There were Indian uprisings in Texas during Houston's first term as governor. But the big problem was the slavery question. The Southern states were threatening secession. Houston's name was mentioned for president of the United States, but the movement for secession was too strong. Some Southern states were gathering arms and preparing for war.

Houston spoke with some of his friends about secession.

"All this talk about secession is disloyal. Even if Mr. Lincoln is elected, the Union is worth more than one man! If we have to fight, let it be in the Union for the Constitution," Houston told his friends.

"General Houston, I suppose you know South Carolina's governor is keeping his legislature in session. He wants his state to be the first to secede if Lincoln wins the election!" said one of the group.

"I don't know about being first, but what are the slaves going to do? We'll have slave uprisings all over the nation if that man wins," added another man.

"And those darned Yankees are setting fires in

many of our towns. People are crazy with fear," said the first man. "We're in for a lot of trouble if he wins."

"We'll have to remain calm. That's the only way we can solve this problem. Fear will get us nowhere," Houston answered.

The governor and his wife were together in Austin when the final election returns came in. In many of the counties the Lone Star flag of the Republic was raised over the courthouses. Things became very tense in Texas. Only four days after Lincoln's election, a group came to Houston to ask for a special session of the legislature.

"We need to join our sister states. Texas must show her support for a just cause," said one visitor.

"You know that Lincoln's election was legal. Texas must accept it as such," Houston told his visitors. "If in some way after he is in office, he should violate the oath of office, then we would be right in revolting."

"Well, he's not going to stand for secession. He'll give us some cause then," said another man.

"It's better for us to remain a part of the Union for the time being," repeated Houston.

Houston was finally forced into calling the legislature into session. A petition had been circulated in the state that called for election of delegates to a convention for secession. Houston knew they would succeed. The convention was called for January 28, 1861; Houston called the legislature into session on January 21st.

At home Houston told Margaret, "I've done what I can. If Texas will be destroyed, I won't go with her. I can resign when the time is right."

South Carolina seceded first, with the other Southern states following in rapid order. They organized themselves into a Confederacy. A president was elected. Although Houston was against the Confederacy, he did agree to send delegates to the inauguration of the Confederate president, Jefferson Davis of Mississippi.

"Margaret, I've tried to keep Texas in the Union. However, if they are determined to secede, I hope they will consider becoming the Lone Star Republic again," Houston told his wife.

When the convention met in January, Houston begged the members to think of Texas. The long Mexican border was a great danger. Texas would be liable to foreign attacks again. The Mexicans might try to reconquer Texas.

The convention members would not listen to Houston's pleas. They drafted a referendum to be placed before the voters on February 23rd. If approved, it would take effect on March 2nd, the twenty-fifth anniversary of the Texas Declaration of Independence.

On February 23rd Texans voted to secede from the Union. The convention met again at Austin on March 2nd. On March 4th Sam Houston announced officially that his state had seceded from the Union.

"However, this does not mean that Texas will join the Confederacy," Houston added. His speech enraged the members of the legislature. They announced at once that the governor was in error.

"I am afraid you are taking too much for granted," Houston told his opponents. "There is not a word in the referendum that says Texas will join the Confederacy. The people have not approved that move."

Houston knew his words would not stop them. However, he was preparing to defy them once again. He was buying time.

On March 14th the convention adopted a resolution that each man in office must take an oath of allegiance to the Confederacy. George W. Chilton was chosen to tell the governor that he had until noon of the 16th to take the oath.

That evening the Houston family had their dinner as usual. After the Negro servants had cleared away the meal, Margaret brought the family Bible to the table. The servants sat along the wall of the dining room. The governor opened the Bible to the passage where he had stopped reading the night before. He read a chapter and talked about its meaning. Then the entire group knelt in prayer.

Shortly after their prayers, George W. Chilton arrived. Houston received him in the parlor.

"Governor Houston, I have been asked to tell you that you will be expected to take the oath of allegiance at noon tomorrow," Chilton said.

"Mr. Chilton, I'm afraid that the time is too short," Houston answered. "I cannot make a decision like that in so little time."

"Well, Sir, could you let the convention know your decision by Saturday noon?" said the uncomfortable visitor. "Then we can make arrangements for your oath at some later date?"

Houston knew what his decision would be, but he needed time to plan his actions. He worried about what his refusal might mean to his family. Tempers in Texas were high. Property had been seized. He couldn't endanger the lives of his wife and eight children.

After he had let Chilton out the door, he kissed Margaret and the children. Upstairs, he removed his coat and shoes. He needed time to think. He could not take that oath. It was against everything he had fought for. He walked the floor most of the evening.

When he went downstairs, Margaret was waiting to hear his decision.

"Mr. Houston, have you made up your mind? What are you going to do?" asked Margaret.

"I will never do it, Margaret," Houston answered. "I would be going against everything I have always stood for." He put his arms around Margaret and kissed her gently. "We have gone through many bad times before. We can certainly take this one more thing."

"You must do what you think is right, my husband," Margaret said softly. "God will watch over us through this bad time."

Houston went to his study after his talk with Margaret. He spent most of the night working on the speech that he intended to give to the people. He had to tell them why he would not take the oath. It was almost dawn before he put out the lights in his study.

Before he could leave for the Capitol building, a message arrived. He would not be given more time for his decision. He must take the oath at noon this very day. The time had come.

Houston opened the basement door to the Capitol. He did not go to his office or report his presence to the officials. He sat down and pulled out his knife to begin whittling. Up above there was a large crowd of excited people. He had no intention of joining them.

Upstairs the secretary announced that all persons whose names were called would take the oath at once.

"Sam Houston!"

Houston heard, but he just continued whittling. Then came a second call.

"Sam Houston!"

Each time his name was called, Houston shaved off another sliver of pine slab. By this time a group of his friends had learned where he was. They gathered around his chair.

Only one other member of the government refused to take the oath. Secretary of State Cave did not answer when his name was called. Justice Roberts called the convention into session. They passed an ordinance that declared the offices of governor and secretary of state to be vacant. Lieutenant Governor Edward Clark took over the government. A successor for Cave would be named.

While this business was being completed, Houston was in his office. He was still working on his address to the people. The convention hoped that they could stop his giving the talk. Finally, on Tuesday, March 18, 1861, Houston sent in his message. The bitterness continued. The convention managers decided that the deposed governor must leave the executive mansion within twenty-four hours.

Friends of the Houstons came in to help the family pack its belongings. After they were through, some of Houston's supporters came to tell him that they were prepared to fight to save his cause. They would send the convention home and reinstate him in office.

Houston could see the future better than they. Armed conflict would not save Texas this time. He knew that Texas had seceded. His loyalty would return to Texas. He hoped that someday he could take Texas out of the Confederacy. He would run up the Lone Star flag over a republic once again. But in the meantime he would be a good citizen of Texas.

The Houstons went home to Independence in May, 1861. Houston passed his time quietly. He had only a few more years to live. Sam Houston, Jr. enlisted in the war against his father's advice. However, Houston was proud of his son, who was wounded at Shiloh.

As Houston grew more and more feeble, the family decided to move back to Huntsville. They acquired a place called "Steamboat House" because of its unusual shape. Margaret remained at Houston's side constantly, reading his favorite passages from the Bible to him. On Sunday evening, July 26, 1863, Sam Houston died in his sleep.

BIBLIOGRAPHY

Braider, Donald, *Solitary Star, a Biography*, New York, G. P. Putnam Sons, 1974.

Day, Donald, and H. H. Ullom, eds., *The Autobiography of Sam Houston*, Norman, University of Oklahoma, 1954.

"Dr. Burleson's Interesting Account of Sam Houston Marriage," *Houston Daily Post*, September 11, 1900.

Foreman, Grant, *Indian Removal*, Norman, University of Oklahoma Press, 1972.

Francis, Ruth Garrison, "Sam Houston's Home Now State Museum," *Dallas Morning News*, May 5, 1929.

Friend, Llerena, *Sam Houston, The Great Designer*, Austin, University of Texas Press, 1954.

Gregory, Jack, and Rennard Strickland, *Sam Houston with the Cherokees, 1829-1833*, Austin, University of Texas Press, 1967.

Hamilton, Jeff (as told to Lenoir Hunt), *My Master*, Dallas, Manfred Van Nort and Company, 1940.

Herz, Lillian E., "Sam Houston's Isle Speech," *Galveston Daily News*, July 21, 1963.

Hightower, Rebecca, "General Sam Houston's Daughter Relates New Facts," *Houston Chronicle*, April 22, 1923.

Hunter, E. C., "Sam Houston Was Indians' Friend," *Galveston Daily News*, March 13, 1921.

James, Bessie Rowland and Marquis James, *6 Feet 6*, New York, Bobbs-Merrill Company, Inc., 1931.

James, Marquis, *The Raven*, Georgia, Norman S. Berg, 1929. (by arrangement with Bobbs-Merrill Company).

Littlejohn, E. G., "Houston Was Stormy Petrel," *Galveston Daily News* (clipping found in Rosenberg Library, Galveston).

Moore, John Trotwood, "Houston, The Greatest Comeback in American History," *Saturday Evening Post*, May 19, 1928.

Raines, C. W., ed., *Year Book for Texas*, Vol. II, 1901, pp. 451-452.

Seale, William, *Sam Houston's Wife*, Norman, University of Oklahoma Press, 1970.

Shuffler, R. Henderson, "The day 'ol Sam stole Lamar's thunder," *Houston Post*, October 16, 1966.

Smith, Dr. W. R. L., *The Story of the Cherokees*. Cleveland, Tennessee, The Church of God Publishing House, 1928.

Starkey, Marion L., *The Cherokee Nation*, New York, Alfred A. Knopf, 1946.

Turner, Martha Anne, *Sam Houston and His Twelve Women*, Austin, The Pemberton Press, 1966.

Williams, Amelia, *Following General Sam Houston*, Austin, Steck Company, 1935.

Wisehart, M. K., *Sam Houston, American Giant*, Washington, Robert B. Luce, Inc., 1962.

Winfrey, Dorman H., "The Texan Archives War of 1842," *The Southwestern Historical Quarterly*. October 1960, pp. 412-427

Statue Honoring
General Sam Houston

Copy is a letter to Texas President General Houston from U.S. President Andrew Jackson.

Private correspondence
Hermitage
Janry 19th, 1844

Genl Saml Houston
  President of Texas.

  My Dear Sir,
    I wrote you yesterday, which I hope has reached you on the subject of annexation of Texas to the United States — I have no hesitation to say to you that it is all important for the future prosperity of Texas and the United States that this should be the result.
    I have recd this morning from our mutual friend R. I. Walker of the Senate of the United States from Mississippi a letter which I enclose you. There are great anxiety with the democratic party in Congress that this annexation should now take place during the present session of Congress. You must recollect how anxious I was, when your independence was acknowledge, to meet your commissioners on this subject, which brought out that old fire-brand J. Q. Adams against it. You will see from Mr. Walkers letter that it is confidential and you will please, when read and noted to burn it — You will find how sanguine Mr. Walker is of the confirmation of the treaty by the Senate if made. You know and can rely on my friendship. I say to you that such a treaty made under your administration will be doing more for the prosperity & permanent happiness of Texas, and redound more to your popularity than any other act of your life, and will prostrate all your enemies. I am exhausted and can write no more — God bless you & yours & grant you prosperity in this life & the life to come is the prayer of your friend —
                                    Andrew Jackson

Private & confidential Hermitage
                              Jany 19th 1844
Genl. Saml. Houston
    President of Texas.
        My dear sir,
            I wrote you yesterday
which I hope has reached you, on the
subject of annexation of Texas to the
United States — I have no hesitation to
say to you that it is all important
for the future prosperity of Texas
& the United States that this should
be the result.

        I have rec'd this morning from
our mutual friend R. I. Walker of the
Senate of the United States, from
Mississippi a letter which I enclose you —
with the Democratic party in Congress
that this annexation should now
take place during the present session
of Congress. you must recollect how
anxious I was, when your independence
was acknowledged, to meet your com-
missioners on this subject, which
brought out that old firebrand J. Q.
Adams against it. you will see from
Mr. Walkers letter that it is confidential
and you will please, when read one
noted, to burn it. you will find how
sanguine Mr. Walker is of the confirma-
tion of the treaty by the Senate if made
    you know I can rely on my friend-
ship & I say to you that such a treaty

made under your administration will be doing more for the prosperity & permanency of Texas, and redound more to your popularity than any other act of your life, and will prostrate all your enemies. I am exhausted and can write no more — God bless you & yours & grant you prosperity in this life & the life to come is the prayer of your friend.

Andrew Jackson

— "Courtesy Rosenberg Library, Galveston, Texas."